CW01335844

THE LITTLE BOOK OF BLACKROCK

HUGH ORAM

First published 2019

The History Press
The Mill, Brimscombe Port
Stroud, Gloucestershire, GL5 2QG
www.thehistorypress.co.uk

British Library Cataloguing in Publication Data.
A catalogue record for this book is available from the British Library.

ISBN 978 0 7509 8912 1

Typesetting and origination by The History Press
Printed and bound in Great Britain by TJ International Ltd

CONTENTS

ACKNOWLEDGEMENTS

I am especially indebted to my beloved wife Bernadette, who in my forty-year-long book career, has given me infinite help and advice all along the way. I also owe a great debt of gratitude to friends who have been unwavering in their support: Thelma Byrne, Dublin; Christina Cannon, Dublin; Aisling Curley, Dublin; Miriam Doyle, Blackrock, Co Dublin; Maria Gillen, Achill and Athlone; and Mary Murphy, Caherlistrane, Co Galway.

I also much appreciate the help given by Alyson Carney, architecture department, Dún Laoghaire-Rathdown County Council, as well as the council's arts department; Aisling Dunne, Irish Architectural Archive; Stephen Ferguson, assistant secretary, An Post; Aidan Fitzgerald, Blackrock; Christy Hehir, An Post Museum and Archive; Elena T. Koleva, Newtownpark, Blackrock; Martello Press, Blackrock; Myles McWeeney, Sandymount, Dublin; Caroline Mullan, Archives Department, Blackrock College; Gerard O'Connor, Blackhall Publishing; Peter Pearson, Co Wexford; Feargal Quinn; Sharks Committee, St Augustine's School, Blackrock; and Brody Sweeney.

A big thank you, too, to artist Nick Fegan for his excellent line drawings for the book.

I am much indebted, as always, to Dean Lochner of the Bondi Group in Ballsbridge, Dublin, for all his technical help in the production of this book.

INTRODUCTION

What is now the upmarket seaside suburb of Blackrock, in south Co Dublin, one of the most elegant as well as one of the most expensive places to live in the Dublin area, was once known as Newtown. It was known as such from the fifteenth century and the name wasn't changed until the early seventeenth century. But the Newtown name lives on in the Newtownpark Avenue area of Blackrock, whose name was derived from the large outcrop of limestone found on the seashore. It's known locally as calp and it turns black when wet. Some historical sources say that the name came from one large lump of limestone in the sea, just off the strand in Blackrock, that turned black when it got wet.

For some four centuries, Blackrock was little more than a name on the map; it was open country, running down to the seashore, but little if any development took place that would merit the name of a settlement. The first village here was on the seashore between Blackrock and Seapoint; until the eighteenth century this was called Newtown on the Strand. It wasn't until the eighteenth century that various wealthy families, almost entirely Protestant, decided to build great houses in the area, such as Frescati House, shamefully demolished in 1983 and now the site of the Frascati Shopping Centre.

In the eighteenth century, the Blackrock area first became a fashionable holiday, bathing and health resort for many of the gentry and other wealthy citizens who lived in Dublin.

They could enjoy the clean sea air as an antidote to the polluted, overcrowded and unhealthy living conditions of Dublin city. They came to Blackrock, where they were in the habit of building elegant seaside villas, with small but well-planted estates attached. Ironically, since then, contemporary Blackrock has largely turned its back on the sea.

The first big boost for Blackrock came in December 1834, when the first railway line in Ireland, indeed the world's first commuter railway, opened. It ran from Westland Row in Dublin, now Pearse station, to what was then the seaside village of Dunleary. Blackrock Station was opened when the railway started, and the new form of travel meant that, for the first time, people could live in Blackrock and travel easily into the city centre. By 1843, just five years after the arrival of the railway, Blackrock had a well-developed town structure. The great commuting tradition had begun in earnest and it is still very important in the town today, using the DART electric trains as opposed to the steam locos used on the line from its beginning until the 1960s.

While Blackrock began to develop as a dormitory suburb of Dublin, the rich and famous continued to flock there and build a tremendous array of big houses. Some of them still survive today, especially along thoroughfares such as Cross Avenue, while many others have been adapted for other purposes, like the great late-eighteenth-century Newtownpark House, which is now a nursing home.

Many Blackrock residents who joined the British armed forces during the First World War were killed in action and their loss had an adverse effect on the development of Blackrock's business community. But by the 1870s, the village started to develop, with those developments mainly centred around the Main Street area.

As the population grew, to its present level of around 25,000, so too did the retail opportunities. From the middle of the nineteenth century, Main Street was the primary place to shop in Blackrock – indeed the only place to shop – with celebrated shops like Findlaters grocery and off licence. Today, Main Street is still going strong, transformed by the infusion of many restaurants as well as modern-day shops. But the mid-1980s saw the construction of the Blackrock Shopping Centre, spearheaded by Superquinn, while following the demolition (in highly controversial circumstances) of Frescati House, Roches Stores also came to Blackrock. Eventually, this evolved into the Frascati Shopping Centre. A major extension of this development is due to be ready in 2019, along with the completed refurbishments at the Blackrock Shopping Centre (now simply known as the Blackrock Centre) across the road, where the anchor tenant is Super Valu, the successor to Superquinn.

Many religious institutions once had substantial interests in property in the Blackrock area, but by now they have almost completely sold these on. Many new houses and apartments have been built on land once owned in the area by religious institutions. Blackrock has also seen many large office buildings constructed.

Despite a concentration of commuter housing in Blackrock, as well as the development of retail outlets and the construction of office blocks, the district has managed to maintain a keen interest in the arts and and has remained attractive for people in the creative sector, such as writers and painters. Even James Joyce lived in Blackrock for a short while as a boy, one of his many addresses in the Dublin area. Blackrock has also built up a tremendous reputation for its bookshops, with present-day outlets such as Raven Books and Dubray Books making a significant contribution.

Over the years, Blackrock has attracted many well-known people in Irish life as residents, including the likes of Liam Devally, the TV star turned judge. It has had more than its fair share of characters, too, from Johnny the hobo who endlessly traversed Rock Road during the 1970s, to Dr John Fleetwood, founder of a noted medical practice in Blackrock and who also had a remarkable parallel career in broadcasting. Blackrock has also distinguished itself in medicine, through the Blackrock Clinic.

In educational terms also, from Blackrock College to UCD's Michael Smurfit Graduate Business School, Newtown Comprehensive School and the new further education facilities in its heart, Blackrock has long been regarded as one of the districts in Ireland with the widest spread of top-class establishments, from primary right through to third level and postgraduate.

Not all the changes have been entirely for the better. The Blackrock bypass, opened in 1988, was necessary to divert through traffic away from Main Street, but it had the effect of cutting Blackrock in two and separating most of it from the Main Street area. Blackrock has also largely managed to turn its back on the sea and the Blackrock Baths came to an ignominious end in 2012; they have never been replaced with successor facilities. It also has to be said that much of the recent architecture in Blackrock, especially its series of office blocks, shows little design merit and even less integration with its surroundings.

But having said all that, Blackrock remains a district of distinction, a place that is still as fiercely proud of its identity as when it had its own town council.

1

TIMELINE

1488: Present-day Blackrock called Newtown in parliamentary legislation. It and a vast area on the outskirts of Dublin were controlled by the Cistercians of St Mary's Abbey, off present-day Capel Street in Dublin

1610: At around this date, the name of the area was changed from Newtown to Blackrock

1659: What is now Blackrock had twelve residents, two English and ten Irish

1739: Frescati House built

1824: Carmelite chapel opened in what is now Sweetman's Lane.

1834: Westland Row to Dunleary railway line opened, including Blackrock station

1839: Blackrock baths opened beside the railway station

1845: St John the Baptist Catholic church opened in Blackrock

1860: Blackrock Town Commissioners established

1863: Seapoint Railway Station opened

1865: Blackrock Town Hall completed

1804: Work started on Martello Tower at Williamstown

1873: Blackrock Park created

1899: St Andrew's Presbyterian church, Mount Merrion Avenue, opened

1905: Carnegie Library and Technical Institute opened

1967: Guardian Angels' Catholic church on Newtownpark Avenue opened

1973: RTÉ television and radio presenter Ryan Tubridy born in Booterstown, but grew up in Blackrock

1983: Frescati House demolished, despite widespread protests; what is now the Frascati Shopping Centre built on site

1984: Blackrock Shopping Centre opened, with Superquinn, now Super Valu

1986: Blackrock Clinic opened

1988: Blackrock bypass opened

1988: Blackrock postal sorting office, Carysfort Avenue, opened

1991: UCD Michael Smurfit Graduate Business School opened in present location in Blackrock

1996: Blackrock Market opened, just off Main Street

2003: The old post office in Main Street closed down; business transferred to the Frescati Shopping Centre

2

ANCIENT ROADS AND OLD BUILDINGS

NO. 1, AVOCA AVENUE

This two-storey over-basement house, built sometime before 1850, is typical of the many villas and houses built in Blackrock during the mid- to late-nineteenth century. It was also very capacious, with no fewer than nine bedrooms. For some sixty years in the later twentieth century, it was the home of the Stephenson family, Desmond Stephenson and his family; he was a brother of the renowned Dublin architect, Sam Stephenson. In his time there, visitors included Brendan Behan, the writer, and another writer, Brian O'Nolan, otherwise known as Flann O'Brien, who lived three doors away.

BLACKROCK HOUSE

Blackrock House in Newtown Avenue was built as a two-storey Georgian house in about 1774; its third storey was added later. Unusually for the time, the facade of the house was faced in red brick. Most houses built in that period had their facades rendered. The house was indeed spacious, with six reception rooms and eight family bedrooms, two servants' rooms, a servants' hall, a laundry, a bootroom, and wine and beer cellars. The grounds ran down to the seashore and included a walled garden and grass tennis courts. An octagon summer house stood on the shore below the garden and the ruins of it are still there today.

The house was connected with several newsworthy and sometimes tragic events. In 1789, two young men, Crosbie and Maguire, ascended in a balloon from Mount Pleasant Square in Ranelagh. The ascent was successful but when they attempted to bring the balloon down, it landed in the sea off Howth. The two were rescued and taken across Dublin Bay to Blackrock House, where they were duly entertained. More tragically, in November 1807, when the *Prince of Wales* ran aground near Blackrock House, many of the bodies of soldiers, rescued from the stricken vessel, were laid out in Blackrock House.

Among the occupiers in the first eighty years of its existence were Lord Rutland and the Marquis of Buckingham. The last single owner-occupier of the house was the McCormick family, who bought it in 1898. They sold the house and the surrounding land in 1935; by 1940, it had been converted into flats, while part of the grounds were bought by a building firm called Archers, which built the terraced and semi-detached houses still standing today. At present, Blackrock House remains standing and is used for social housing.

CARYSFORT AVENUE

By 1840, the lower part of Carysfort Avenue had been fully developed, with some of the houses built in terraces, all distinguished by attractive door cases and fanlights. The terraces here were very similar in design to those at Prince of Wales Terrace, also on Carysfort Avenue. Close by, Anglesea Avenue and Sydney Avenue had been built earlier, about 1830, with late-Georgian-style terraced houses.

CARYSFORT PARK

Now owned by University College, Dublin, Carysfort House was built in 1803 by Sir John Proby and leased to Judge William Saurin, a notable legal figure of the time. Carysfort Park was built as a large three-storey over-basement house with a fine portico. The house was surrounded by open fields, which in recent times have been built over with houses and apartments. The house and the estate were bought by the Sisters of Mercy in 1891, who ran an industrial school for children there until 1903, when a teacher training college for women was set up. In this college, Éamon de Valera was an early professor of mathematics, appointed in 1906.

Other old buildings in Carysfort College included the novitiate, the halls of residence and the old farm buildings. Subsequently, newer buildings included the College of Education and a sports hall. In 1989, the Sisters of Mercy put their convent and the teacher training college on the market and Carysfort Park subsequently housed UCD's graduate school of business studies.

DESTRUCTION OF OLD HOUSES

Over the past fifty years, since the late 1960s, the huge demand for building land in the Blackrock area has resulted in the destruction of many fine old houses, houses that once had considerable architectural and historical appeal. Artist and conservationist writer Peter Pearson has chronicled the destruction of many of these old houses, including Frescati House, Maretimo, Rosefield, Fitzwilliam Lodge, Laurel Hill, Elm Cliff, Dawson Court, Villa Nova, The Elms, Lisalea,

Cherbury, Sans Souci, Rockville, Ardagh Park, Ardlui, Carysfort, Talbot Lodge, Hawthorn, Clareville and the eighteenth-century stables at Newtownpark House.

Some houses were saved from destruction, such as South Hill and the old house which is the focal point of the Blackrock Market, thanks to the interventions of An Taisce, even though planning permission had been given that allowed for their destruction.

DUNARDAGH

This fine house in the Italianate style was built at Temple Hill in 1860 and was complemented by its fine gardens. It subsequently became a seminary run by the Daughters of Charity. Nearby was Craigmore, built slightly earlier in the more restrained Georgian style, for a wealthy Quaker tea merchant called Jonathan Hogg. Subsequently, it became a centre for mentally handicapped people. Also close by was one of the finest Victorian mansions in Blackrock, Ardlui, also built in the Italianiate style. It had a very large conservatory running the full length of its south front and it was noted for its fine gardens. Sadly, this fine house was demolished in 1955.

FORT LISLE, ELM CLIFF AND VAUXHALL GARDENS

Two houses, known as Vauxhall Gardens and Elm Cliff, were built around 1750 for a Dublin brewer called William Medcalf. They had spectacular sea views and were also renowned for their gardens. Vauxhall Gardens was converted into a hotel in 1793, while in 1834, Elm Cliff, formerly Fort Lisle, was turned into a boarding house. In 1879, Elm Cliff's land was incorporated into the then new People's Park, while the house itself was demolished in 1880. The other house, Vauxhall Gardens, suffered a similar fate, but today the gates that once formed its entrance are at the entrance to the park, while the gardens of the two houses are still incorporated into the grounds.

HAWTHORN

This large Victorian house was built about 1850 on a field adjacent to Carysfort Avenue; among its outstanding features was a large porch with a flight of granite steps and a pair of old gas lamps. The house was demolished in 1987 and the grounds were then completely built over.

LINDEN

Linden, in the area where Blackrock meets Stillorgan, was built around an eighteenth-century villa. Linden was run as a convalescent home for well over a century, from 1864 until 1996. The home was begun and run by the Sisters of Charity, who had also set up St Vincent's Hospital. The third house here, Talbot Lodge, was also run as part of that convalescent home. Linden was also renowned for its gardens. The houses were eventually demolished and the site redeveloped for housing.

LIOS AN UISCE

At the bottom of Mount Merrion Avenue, in the mid-eighteenth century, a merchant and brewer called William Medcalf leased several plots from the Fitzwilliam Estate, the predecessor of the Pembroke Estate, in order to build a number of fine houses. He was obliged by the terms of his lease to spend at least £300 on each house and to make considerable plantations of trees such as oak and elm.

One of the houses he built is now known as Lios an Uisce, or Lisnaskea, on the high ground overlooking what is now Blackrock Park. In its first incarnation, the house, then known as Peafield Cliff, was of simple design, two storeys high and five windows wide. In 1754, it was leased to Lady Arabella Denny, along with two adjacent fields that would later become the site of Sion Hill convent and Peafield Terrace at the foot of Mount Merrion Avenue.

As the house didn't have enough room for the large gatherings that assembled to dine and dance, in the tradition of Georgian Ireland, Lady Arabella had substantial extensions built on to the house, while she also had laid out a fine landscaped garden.

MARETIMO

Maretimo was built as a marine villa in about 1770 by Sir Nicholas Lawless, MP for Lifford in Co Donegal, and a successful woollen merchant, otherwise known as Lord Cloncurry. Like the neighbouring villas, Maretimo was renowned for its constant entertainments, at all hours of the day and night, and its lavish garden parties. Sir Nicholas was also a keen collector of classical antiquities and a generous patron of the arts. After he died in 1799, his second son, Valentine, succeeded him, and when the railway line from Westland Row to Dunleary was being built, it was he who persuaded the railway company to build an elaborate bridge, the Cloncurry Towers, which are still in place over the line.

With the death of the fourth baron in the early 1930s, the title died out. The 1936 Ordnance Survey map shows new terraced and two-storey houses that had been built in the former gardens of Maretimo House by a developer called J.P. Colbert. The big house itself survived until 1970, when it was demolished and replaced with an apartment block.

MELFIELD

Melfield, which is now in the grounds of Newpark Comprehensive School on Newtownpark Avenue, was built in the late eighteenth century, but little of the once elaborate interior survived. For many years, prior to the establishment of Newpark School, the house was occupied by the Avoca and Kingstown Junior School. Also nearby was Belfort, a solid Victorian house built in 1870. The gardens of this house were used to create all-weather playing pitches.

MOUNT MERRION AVENUE

Mount Merrion Avenue, which runs straight as a die downhill from the Stillorgan Road to the main road at Blackrock for a distance of 2km, dates back to the earlier eighteenth century.

At that stage, the Fitzwilliam family had their main residence at Mount Merrion; in 1704, Richard Fitzwilliam became the fifth Viscount Fitzwilliam and promptly built Mount Merrion House. Mount Merrion Avenue started out as the avenue on the eastern approaches to the big house. Both this and the adjoining Cross Avenue were laid out as just a small part of the overall grandiose landscaping plan for the whole estate.

Until about 1800, Mount Merrion Avenue was almost entirely undeveloped, but as the nineteenth century unfolded, so too did housing development begin. Seven plain-looking houses were built at Pembroke Terrace, on the lower part of the road, while Peafield Terrace was built opposite. In the nineteenth and earlier twentieth century, further infill developments were built along Mount Merrion Avenue, including the near contemporary Brookfield and Brooklawn.

NEWTOWNPARK

Below what was once the Playwright pub in Newtownpark Avenue and the present-day small shopping centre, there was once a continuous row of small terraced houses that made up the village of Newtownpark. But these days, virtually all trace of them has disappeared, including the cottages off Price's Lane.

NEWTOWNPARK HOUSE

Newtownpark House, just off Newtownpark Avenue, was built in 1770 in the classical style for Ralph Ward on an existing site. Ward was the surveyor-general of ordnance and he died at Newtownpark House in 1788. During the nineteenth century,

the house had a number of owners, including John Armit, a wealthy army agent, who bought it in 1805. In 1946, Senator E.A. McGuire bought the house; the McGuire family were the then-owners of the old Brown Thomas department store in Grafton Street, Dublin. Much of the McGuire family's collection of fine art in the house was sold off by auction in 1976.

In 1984, the house and its remaining gardens (much of the estate had been sold off for housing development between 1967 and 1972) were sold to what became the Newtownpark House nursing home. It opened in 1987 and still occupies the house today.

OLD BATHS

Blackrock has long been renowned as a swimming place, and John Rocque's 1757 map of the Dublin area showed that what is now Blackrock had baths for women close to the rock from which the area took its name, according to many sources, and also close to what became Blackrock's swimming pool. In the eighteenth century, there were also separate baths for men in the area now covered by Blackrock Park.

Also in the eighteenth century, what is now Blackrock was renowned for its places of entertainment, such as the one at Castle Byrne, close to where Newtown Avenue and Seapoint Avenue now meet. One pamphleteer of the time was unimpressed by the general throng of dubious individuals and by what he called the 'scabby parcel of pygmy tents' that were set up to cater for people in search of entertainment. He also said that strong drink was freely available and gave the impression that, as a result, morals were loose.

PEMBROKE HOUSE

This rather plain house was built about 1830. Jonathan Goodbody, a Dublin stockbroker who came to live here in the 1880s, added a two-storey, bow-fronted extension and an elaborate granite doorcase. The house, at the bottom of Mount Merrion Avenue, now houses the Benincasa School.

PROBY SQUARE

The first proposal to build what became Proby Square, off Carysfort Avenue, came in 1840, but the square never materialised. By 1843, only four tall houses had been built on the north side but curiously, the short cul-de-sac is still called Proby Square. The Church of All Saints was built here in 1868 and close by, in 1875, the Meath Protestant Industrial School for Boys was set up to house homeless children and children who had committed minor offences. At its busiest, it accommodated 150 boys.

ROCKFIELD HOUSE

Rockfield House was built at Newtownpark Avenue in the 1750s and in its heyday it had extensive grounds. For the rest of the eighteenth century, this was the most important big house in the area.

The design of the house was French and even though many alterations and enlargements have been made to it, the original design can still be clearly made out. In 1772, Lord Townsend, towards the end of his vice-royalty in Ireland, chose Rockfield House as his summer residence. It became renowned for its dissolute parties, full of fun and revelry. It eventually passed to Sir Boyle Roche, who was master of ceremonies at Dublin Castle.

For most of the nineteenth century, from about 1840 until around 1890, the house was owned by the Valentine O'Brien O'Connor/Henchy family. The house was then sold to William Geoghegan, the chief engineer in the Guinness brewery, who lived there until 1930. He was responsible for adding the huge ugly wing on to the house, which still dominates Newtownpark Avenue.

Rockfield House had first been used to provide medical services during the First World War, when the Geoghegan family turned over part of the house for use by wounded or invalided soldiers. In the 1950s, the Sisters of Mercy set up a private female psychiatric hospital in the house and called it Cluain Mhuire. By 1995, Cluain Mhuire was providing these services to both children and adults.

ROCKVILLE

In the nineteenth century Rockville, at the bottom of Newtownpark Avenue, long since demolished, was home to Thomas Bewley. It was also renowned for its gardens and its tropical greenhouses. Behind Rockfield, Dunardagh was built about 1860 in the extravagant Italian style. This house once had a magnificent pair of granite entrance gates that were subsequently relocated close to the Blackrock bypass. In 1939, the Daughters of Charity took over the house to run St Catherine's Seminary there.

ST ANNE'S SQUARE

This local authority housing, just off Temple Road, has a design that is unique to Blackrock. Built just over 120 years ago, in red brick, this three-storey block is noted for its metal balconies and exterior staircases. St Anne's Close, opposite, consists of more modern housing.

The original houses here were built in 1897: three-storey, two-storey and one-storey artisans' houses. They were built for the Blackrock town commissioners and were designed by an architectural practice called Millar & Symes. It was founded in 1874 and was eventually run by the Millar family until it closed down in 1966. At the time these houses were designed, the practice was based in Great Brunswick Street, now Pearse Street, Dublin. It also did a lot of design work for the Bank of Ireland.

The flats in St Anne's Square were substantially refurbished and upgraded by the county council in 1998. Extensions were built to the rear of the block to facilitate new kitchens and bathrooms, while the deck access and stairways were also upgraded. Other local authority housing in the area includes Frascati Court, on the main Blackrock bypass, which opened in 1986.

TRAMWAY COTTAGES

To the east of Blackrock village and facing Newtown Avenue, there was once a tram depot, converted into a garage and car showrooms in the 1960s. Beside the tram depot, cottages were built for the tramway workers. The cottages are still there today, known as Newtown Villas.

The first tram depot had been built in about 1885 on the former walled gardens of Maretimo House. The tramway cottages weren't built until much later, around 1909, and while the trams were still in existence, the cottages were occupied by either tramway workers or widows of these workers. The widows usually took in boarders, who in turn were generally tramway workers, so the connection between the tram depot and the adjacent cottages continued until the trams closed down in 1949.

These cottages were very similar in style to the cottages that the Dublin United Tramways Company built beside its other depots across the city. The cottages at Newtown Avenue cost about £150 to build; they were single-storey, constructed from red brick, and with a central porch that had windows on either side. All the plans and drawings of Dublin's tramway cottages were destroyed when the headquarters of the tramway company was blown up in 1922, during the civil war. The design of the trams was influenced to some extent by the Arts and Crafts movement popular at the time of their construction.

Shortly after Ireland's national transport system CIE was formed in 1945 to take over the tramway company and the main railways, the cottages were sold off, with the name being changed to Newtown Villas.

WALTHAM TERRACE

This elegant road of terraced houses just off Mount Merrion Avenue was constructed in 1836 at a time when it was commonplace for Portland stone to be used for these villa-type houses. No. 1, Waltham Terrace was built at this time and in 1994, builder and developer Noel Rhatigan bought the house. He rebuilt half of the three-storey house – one of the few detached houses built in Waltham Terrace – and completely refurbished the rest. The house was put on the market in 2017 with an asking price of close on €2 million.

WILLIAMSTOWN

These days, the small village of Williamstown, on the main road between Booterstown and Blackrock, is often considered to be part of Blackrock.

Back in 1848, when Williamstown was considered a village in its own right, it was described as occupying 18 hectares, with a population of 575 living in ninety-four houses. At that stage, its days as a popular bathing place on the shores of Dublin Bay had largely faded away, although people were still coming to Williamstown to bathe there. It also had hot and cold saltwater baths, and even had its own police station, run by the Dublin Metropolitan Police.

In 1848, it was stated that numerous jaunting cars stopped at Williamstown on their way to and from Dublin, Blackrock and Kingstown, now Dún Laoghaire. Williamstown also had its own railway station, but it only lasted for six years. It opened in 1835, shortly after the Westland Row to Dunleary railway opened, and closed for the last time on 10 May 1841.

Very unusually, the whole village of Williamstown was physically shifted from one side of Rock Road to the other in around 1909. Blackrock College was carrying out major expansions; Williamstown, up until then, had been based on that side of Rock Road, but all the houses, pubs and shops there were demolished and rebuilt on the far side of the road.

3

CHURCHES

ALL SAINTS CHURCH

All Saints Church of Ireland church, together with its rectory, face on to Proby Square, at the top of Carysfort Avenue. The road on which it is set was built up between 1840 and 1880, and the church itself is very attractive, with unusual features.

It consists of a nave, side aisles and a tower with a short spire. It also has a square apse and transept. The main windows in the nave are triangular in shape, a very unusual feature, while there are large clerestory windows, which provide most of the light. Both the church and the rectory, which is to the rear of the church, were built from granite. In recent times, the parish of All Saints has been amalgamated with that in Stillorgan (St Brigid's), but services are still held in both churches.

CHRIST CHURCH

Christ Church was the oldest church in Blackrock; it was built by the Rev Thomas Kelly (1769–1854), who founded the Kellyite sect as a breakaway from the Church of Ireland. He also wrote a number of hymns.

The church was built on Carysfort Avenue, close to the present day junction with the Blackrock bypass and on the same side of the street as the Black Horse pub. Although the church opened in the early nineteenth century as a dissenting chapel, it was eventually brought back within the Church of Ireland fold, which it joined in 1872. It remained in use as a Church of Ireland church until it closed in March 1960, despite a lengthy legal battle by the parishioners who fought unsuccessfully to keep it open. The tall building was demolished the following year. Parts of the external railings survived for many years, while the organ was transferred to the Sacred Heart church in Donnybrook.

CHURCH OF THE GUARDIAN ANGELS

This church, on Newtownpark Avenue, is by far the newest in Blackrock, since its construction only started in the mid-1960s.

The whole area of Newtownpark saw much development during that decade, with a lot of new housing developments, so a new parish was created from the existing one of St John the Baptist in Blackrock.

The Sisters of Charity made the land available both for the new church and the adjoining school. The site was blessed and the first sod turned on 17 January 1965. The completed church was blessed and opened by the then Catholic Archbishop of Dublin, Most Rev John Charles McQuaid, on 5 November 1967.

Designed in a very modern style by Charles Ellison, its copper fleche and cross rise to a height of 33.5m. The design of the church had been completed before the Second Vatican Council, so it was subsequently revised and the high altar was repositioned so that Mass could be celebrated facing the laity.

The main exterior finishes on the church are natural concrete and rendering, while inside, the main walls are finished with plaster and a natural concrete finish. The theme of the main stained glass by the front entrance is of the Guardian Angel. The design of the head was copied from that of Cleopatra as played by Elizabeth Taylor in the 1963 film of that name.

Next to the church, the parish centre can seat eighty people, and one of its features is a coffee dock, so that parishioners can come in after Mass for coffee and confectionery. The local community centre is also close by, beside the Wishing Well pub on Newtownpark Avenue.

EARLIEST CATHOLIC CHURCH

The earliest Catholic church in Blackrock was the chapel in the grounds of the Carmelite convent on what was then Chapel Lane, now Sweetman's Avenue. This site subsequently became the Blackrock Hospice. The chapel in Chapel Lane was built in 1824 with money raised by the then parish priest of Booterstown; the Carmelities had arrived in Blackrock two years earlier, in 1822. The new chapel remained the only Catholic church in Blackrock until the church of St John the Baptist opened in 1845.

FORMER METHODIST CHURCH

The former Methodist church at George's Avenue in Blackrock was one of the first built in Ireland, in 1847, following a visit to Ireland by John Wesley. The church, known as the Meeting Hall, was home to the local Methodist congregation for many years, but with dwindling numbers, the Methodist church put the building up for sale in 2001. Subsequently, the building was used as the base for three architectural practices, those of Robin Mandal, Cathal Crimmins and Justin O'Callaghan. In 2016 the three companies decided to vacate the premises and put the church up for sale.

QUAKER BURIAL GROUND

Quakers have long had close connections with Blackrock and their burial ground, extending to 2.3 hectares, was opened at Temple Hill, Blackrock, on 6 March, 1860. Previously, Quakers in Dublin had burial grounds at Cork Street and on York Street, just off St Stephen's Green. The land of the latter burial ground was sold in 1805 to the College of Surgeons in Ireland so that they could extend their premises. Today, nothing is left to be seen of either burial ground.

In 1853, the Quakers reached an agreement to purchase a plot of land near Donnybrook, but this deal fell through at the last minute. It took the Quakers five more years to find the new site at Temple Hill and finalise its purchase. It cost £1,000. The first person to be interred there was Hannah Chapman from 3, William Terrace, Booterstown, who had died on 3 March 1860. By 1923, a total of 959 people had been interred there.

Over the years, the burial ground has always been kept in immaculate condition, helped by occasional fundraising appeals. Under the shade of ancient trees, the simple headstones are carved with brief details of the life of the deceased. The gates to the burial ground are also kept locked, so anyone who wants to visit should either email (office@quakers-in-Ireland.ie) or phone (01 495 6889).

ST ANDREW'S PRESBYTERIAN CHURCH

The Presbyterian parish in Blackrock dates back to 1895 and this church was opened in 1899. A Presbyterian congregation had started worshipping in Blackrock Town Hall on 29 July 1894.

The following year, the congregation bought the site for the church, at the foot of Mount Merrion Avenue, for £750. The church itself was built by Patrick Caulfield of Booterstown; the foundation stone was laid on 27 October 1898 and the first service was held on 5 February 1899. The church was designed in an octagonal shape and it has a large tower by the front entrance. The church organ was installed in 1912, with half the cost being met by the Scottish/American philanthropist Andrew Carnegie, who also did much to improve the library service throughout Ireland. A new parish hall was built in 1959, at a cost of £15,000. Rev George Campbell has been the minister from 1986 up to the present day.

ST JOHN THE BAPTIST

The Catholic church close to the centre of Blackrock village had an unusual donor: Valentine Lawless, Second Lord Cloncurry, the son of the first Lord Cloncurry who had built nearby Maretimo House, where the second Lord Cloncurry also lived. Lawless donated the land for the church, which is now dedicated to him. It also has a stained glass window dedicated to him, while he also presented the new parish with a copy of Murillo's *Madonna and Child*.The church itself was designed by Patrick Byrne in 1842. A tablet on the tower, now largely obscured, notes that the church was built in gratitude to the gift of temperance. In those far off days, Fr Mathew's crusades against the evils of drink attracted huge public attention and support.

After the church was built, additions in a plainer style were made in 1850 and 1856, while the most recent extension has been to the west end of the building. The interior is lofty, with imposing period-style vaultings. It has an elaborate Gothic reredos of the Apostles and a Gothic pulpit. Over the door is an entablature of John baptising Christ in the River Jordan. The stained glass windows of the church were made in the Early Studios in Camden Street; the studios also worked with such renowned artists as Evie Hone and Harry Clarke.

4

CRIME AND MAYHEM

BANK RAID

In February 2018, an armed man entered a bank branch on Main Street, Blackrock, and demanded that the staff open the till. One of the bank workers bravely attempted to disarm the would-be robber, who had a pistol, but the robber then fled the scene, having stolen nothing.

BLACKROCK ASSOCIATION

In the late eighteenth century, Blackrock village, as well as the main road from there to Dublin, were notorious for crime. The Blackrock Association was set up in 1782 by noblemen and gentlemen of the district to apprehend, prosecute and convict all persons guilty of housebreaking, highway robbery and other acts of theft and trespass, not only in Blackrock, but in much of south Co Dublin. The association also instigated nightly patrols on the main road from Blackrock to Baggot Street, to prevent highway robbers holding up coaches and robbing the passengers.

FIRE AT BLACKROCK MARKET

Three units at the Blackrock Market, which had been established in 1996, were badly damaged by a fire in the early hours of the morning in November 1998; arson was suspected.

GARDA STATION

The old Garda station, in a building constructed about 1750 just off Main Street, closed down over twenty years ago; the Blackrock Market opened in front of it in 1996. The new Garda station, which backs on to the Blackrock bypass, was built by a private developer and sold to the Office of Public Works.

REVOLVER DUEL

In 1923, the then-owner of Newtown House in Blackrock, J.J. Byrne, heard a strange noise in his garden, which sounded as if someone was going in or out of the house. He discovered two armed men in his garden; one them was stooping low under a window, while the other was at his back. He rushed for his revolver and chased the two men; they both turned round and fired shots at him. One of the bullets just missed his head, piercing a hole in his hat. In return J.J. Byrne fired five shots at the raiders, who escaped in different directions. One went in the direction of Seapoint, while the other made for the nearby main road.

Byrne ran back into the house and phoned Blackrock Garda station. By chance, the assistant commissioner of the Dublin Metropolitan Police was on a visit to the station when the call came in. He set out with a small number of gardaí and they arrived at Newtown House a short while later, to find that the shooting had stopped. J.J. Byrne was unharmed, although a little the worse for his strange experience. The motive behind the incident had obviously been to stage a pre-Christmas raid on the house. The two culprits were eventually traced to Westland Row railway station, now Pearse station.

An equally odd incident took place that same night in Blackrock when a Clery's van was stopped by a masked man brandishing a revolver. The man inspected the inside of the van, then remarked, mysteriously, 'I thought it was a Ford, you may go.'

5

HEALTH

ALZHEIMER SOCIETY OF IRELAND

The Alzheimer Society of Ireland, which provides care and services for people throughout Ireland suffering from Alzheimer's, has its national office at Temple Road in Blackrock. The society also has the Orchard Day and Respite Care Centre at Temple Road, providing eleven respite beds for people suffering from dementia. After severe deficiencies were found at the centre in 2016, it closed down temporarily in January 2017, but was subsequently reopened, run by Mowlam Healthcare.

BLACKROCK CLINIC

When the Blackrock Clinic opened in 1986, it set new standards in private medicine and continues to do so today.

It was co-founded by surgeons Joseph Sheehan, his brother Jimmy, the late Maurice Neligan and a nuclear medicine specialist, George Duffy, as a private hi-tech hospital offering healthcare to private patients. The clinic is also a teaching hospital and is associated with both the Royal College of Surgeons in Ireland and University College, Dublin. It was built on the site of Rosefield House.

Over the years, the Blackrock Clinic has seen considerable expansion. Back in 2008, it announced a €100 million expansion plan over a five-year period, which doubled its capacity by the time it was completed in early 2014. The clinic's accommodation is now all private, ensuite rooms. In 2006 BUPA, the British health insurance company, sold its 56 per cent stake in the clinic, which was taken up by a number of investors including Breccia, which is owned and controlled by Larry Goodman, the beef baron. In recent years, there have been prolonged legal disputes between Dr Joseph Sheehan and Mr Goodman over matters connected with Goodman's investment in the clinic.

Despite these legal differences, the Blackrock Clinic has continued to thrive and now has more than 300 consultants dealing with over forty medical specialities. The four founders had taken significant personal, financial and professional risks to get the Blackrock Clinic established, with no support from

either the government or the VHI health insurance company. The clinic pioneered hi-tech surgical procedures, medical treatments and groundbreaking diagnostics. Subsequently, many of these pioneering measures were introduced into the public health sector.

Among the major investments made in recent times is the new Emergency Department – three times the size of the original one, opened in 2010 – and the new state-of-the-art intensive care unit, the only one in Ireland to have full-time consultants. Another big recent investment has been in a central decontamination unit, to sterilise instruments and prevent the spread of infection. Infection rates at the Blackrock Clinic are very low, the result of the many protocols and initiatives put in place by the clinic. These infection rates are far lower than for most hospitals in the public sector.

Overall, the Blackrock Clinic has made a significant contribution to medical treatment, including surgery, in Ireland during its more than thirty-year existence, and it and Blackrock have become synonymous.

BLACKROCK HOSPICE

The Sisters of Charity founded their first hospice at Harold's Cross in Dublin in 1879, where they have been caring for terminally ill people ever since. The Sisters of Charity have also been based at Sweetman's Avenue in Blackrock, where their religious community has existed for close-on 150 years. The Blackrock Hospice was opened in the grounds in June 2003 and it has been providing specialist palliative care since September that year. The Blackrock Hospice is affiliated to the one in Harold's Cross.

BLACKROCK MEDICAL PRACTICES

Blackrock is home to a number of medical practices. The Blackrock Medical Practice at 62 Newtownpark Avenue has been providing GP services in modern premises for over thirty years and its medical staff include Dr Conor Murphy, Dr John Murphy and Dr Fiona Magee. The Blackrock Medical Clinic at 34 Main Street has also involved with medical care for the past thirty years. The principal is Dr Barbara Kearns, who is the daughter and granddaughter of general practitioners; also practising here are Dr Eva McLarnon and Dr Camille Spears. The Rockcourt Medical Centre is also based on Main Street (No. 40), while the Blackrock Family Practice is at No.41, with Dr Ide Delargy and Dr Orla Halpenny. The Blackrock Medical Centre is based at 2 Frascati Park.

Dr Clement McCrory and his team are based on the Clonkeen Road, as is the Deansgrange Medical Centre team.

The Carysfort Clinic at Proby Square has been going since 1947, when it was founded by the late Dr John Fleetwood Senior. The practice is now run by his son, Dr John Fleetwood Junior, who joined in 1978. Its medical staff include Dr Patrick Duggan, who joined in 1980, and Dr Frank Marmion, who joined in 1996, while the latest to join is Dr Natalia Bratu. Apart from its GP services, its other services include dentistry.

Blackrock also has a number of single general practitioner practices, including Dr Ciara McMahon of the Amaranta family practice in Ardagh Grove, Dr Peter Staunton in Woodland Park, off Mount Merrion Avenue, and Dr Marian McWade in Avoca Avenue.

The Derma Clinic was founded in 1999 by Patricia Molloy and specialises in laser and cosmetic surgery, plastic surgery and liposuction. For many years, it was based on the Rock Road in Blackrock, but is now on the Monkstown Road.

NEIL BOWMAN TRAINING

Neil Bowman Training is based at Brookfield Terrace in Blackrock; his services include total body workout, instruction in golf and other sports, and boxing training.

ELITE FITNESS AND PERFORMANCE ACADEMY

Based at Brookfield Terrace, one of the two long streets of working-class houses off Brookfield Avenue, this organisation trains people who want to become professional personal trainers.

LEMASNEY ORTHODONTICS

This orthodontic practice is based at 45 Rock Road, Blackrock (with another branch in Bray) and it is run by Dr Niall Lemasney and his team. Their slogan is 'get the smile you want'.

PILATES

The Pilates Studio opened in Brookfield Avenue, Blackrock, in October 2017. In addition to running the studio, the owners, Joe and Mary McCarthy, offer life balance advice and run a holistic therarapy centre at their premises.

REFORM PILATES

Based on the third floor of a building at the back of Main Street, there are spectacular views from its windows over Dublin Bay. It has two rooms; in one, studio classes are taught and it's also used for private clients, while the other room is used for group classes.

6

HISTORICAL PLACES AND EVENTS

BAD DAY AT BLACKROCK

When things go wrong, sometimes people in Blackrock will talk about a 'bad day at Blackrock', without realising that this was the title of an early Cinemascope film released in 1955. The thriller starred Spencer Tracy and Robert Ryan.

BLACKROCK BATHS

The first proposal to build swimming baths in Blackrock came as long ago as 1754, but it didn't take practical effect until after the railway line from Westland Row to Dunleary was opened at the end of 1834.

The Blackrock Promenade and Pier Company was set up to develop a promenade and a bathing place in Blackrock after a public outcry that the new railway had cut off access to the sea. The baths soon took shape, opening in 1839, and became a popular spot for people visiting the seaside at Blackrock. As long ago as 1899, a letter writer to *The Irish Times* complained that 'gentlemen get by by wearing a paucity of clothes at the Blackrock Baths'.

In 1887, the baths were rebuilt in concrete, to designs by architect and engineer William Kaye-Parry. Then, in 1924, the local council took them over, in time for the Tailteann Games of 1929. The swimming and diving events took place at Blackrock, so the facilities at the baths were significantly upgraded and included the installation of grandstand timber seating for 1,150 people.

The period from the late 1920s until the late 1960s was the heyday of the baths, which offered an eight-lane, 50m long pool, a 10m and a 3m diving board and also two smaller pools for children. The last time that the baths were used as a public amenity was in the summer of 1986. From 1987 onwards, they were closed, although the Leinster branch of the Irish Water Polo Association did extensive work to make them usuable again, and made private use of the pool. The 10m-high diving platform, however, was put out of use for safety reasons.

The baths were finally demolished in 2012 and, subsequently, the property consortium that owned them leased the site to the local council, but nothing has been done with it since.

Blackrock Baths always managed to keep in the news, but local residents have been saddened that not only were they demolished, but that nothing replaced them. The foundations are still there, but to date, the site has never been redeveloped.

BLACKROCK CROSS

The old market cross at Blackrock has long been one of the most distinctive features of the village.

This cross dates from the eighth or ninth century and it was probably originally used as a burial slab at the Celtic foundation of St Mochanna in Monkstown. In 1678, when Walter Cheevers moved from Monkstown to Blackrock, he brought the cross with him. When his daughter married into the Byrne family, the cross was moved to the edge of the family property in Blackrock, probably some time around 1770, and was used as a boundary marking.

In 1865, huge controversy erupted in Blackrock when proposals emerged to remove the cross. In the end, various parts were taken off the cross, which was put on a pedestal at the top of Main Street. For many years, it stood outside the front of the Central Café, but in 2014 it was moved about 30m across to the far side of Main Street, where it was repositioned outside a branch of the Bank of Ireland, surrounded by some greenery.

The cross also marked part of the boundary of the jurisdiction of the Corporation of Dublin and, until well into the eighteenth century, members of that corporation visited Blackrock and its

cross once a year in full regalia, in a ceremony known as 'riding the franchises' or 'beating the bounds'. The cross used to be much revered by old residents of Blackrock.

Until quite recently, funerals coming from the church of St John the Baptist first headed north along Temple Road, as far as the cross, where the cortege would pause for a short while before retracing its steps to the church and continuing south to Dean's Grange cemetery.

CINEMAS IN BLACKROCK

Blackrock was once renowned for its cinemas.

In the early years of the twentieth century, the Blackrock Restaurant, run at 13 Main Street by Charles Gray, was converted into a picture house. Called the Blackrock Kinematograph Theatre, it opened on 28 February 1914. It was quite substantial and could accommodate 700 patrons. The new cinema was run by Maurice Elliman, who went on to own several cinemas in Dublin city centre. During the 1920s, it was taken over by John Hanna, but he lost it to the bank in circumstances that are all too familiar to modern readers. Hanna owed the bank a lot of money, so in 1929, it foreclosed on the cinema and sold it off.

It was taken over by a man called McEvoy, who had owned a Dublin city centre cinema. Until 1937, he used the former cinema in Blackrock as a bicycle shop and billiard hall. It reopened on 24 February 1938, following major refurnishment and alterations, as the Regent Cinema. Blackrock residents soon nicknamed it The Tunnel because of its long, narrow layout.

The new cinema changed its programmes three times a week and during the 1950s Westerns were very popular; if they featured either John Wayne or Gary Cooper full houses ensued. In its final years, the cinema was owned by Odeon Ireland, which closed it on 25 March 1961 because of decreasing audiences. After its closure, the old cinema housed a shop and later an indoor market, before being demolished. An apartment block and café were then built on the site.

MARITIME TRAGEDIES

In November 1807, two military ships sank in the Blackrock area, with the loss of close to 500 lives.

On 19 November 1807, these ships and others left Dublin port, taking Irish troops to the Napoleonic wars. One of them was a sloop called the *Prince of Wales*. The weather was so bad that she was blown close to Bray Head, then back past what is Dún Laoghaire. She went aground at Merrion Strand and the 120 soldiers who were locked below decks drowned, while there were only a small number of survivors, including Captain Robert Jones.

The other boat, a brig called the *Rochdale*, was slighly larger, but she suffered the same fate at the *Prince of Wales*, blown towards Bray Head and then back again. She struck the rocks near the Martello Tower at Seapoint and broke up. All on board, 265 souls, including forty-two women and twenty-nine children, were lost. Many of the bodies from the wreck of the *Rochdale* were brought to Blackrock House in Newtown Avenue, where they were laid out prior to burial in Carrickbrennan graveyard in Monkstown.

THE OBELISK

At the top of Carysfort Avenue, as it comes into Stillorgan, is one of the finest obelisks in Ireland, built in 1727 by Lord Allen of Stillorgan Park. He had two purposes in mind: firstly, he wanted to commemorate his wife – the plan was that she would eventually be buried there – and secondly, he wanted to provide much-needed local employment during a famine period.

The tall granite obelisk is 17m high and built on a cross-vaulted, rock-covered base. Steep steps enable visitors to climb up and enter a small, domed chamber at the foot of the obelisk, from where they can admire the view. The obelisk was designed by the leading Palladian architect of the time, Edward Lovett Pearce, who had spent much time in Rome, where he had been inspired by a similar obelisk in the Piazza Navona. Pearce also designed such buildings as the Irish Parliament, now a branch of the Bank of Ireland at College Green. Pearce lived in Stillorgan, but he died tragically young, at the age of 33.

As for Lady Allen, after her husband died, she moved to London, where she died in 1758. She was buried there, rather than beneath the oblelisk. Today, the obelisk can still be seen as a feature on the Carysfort Woods housing estate.

7

MODERN HOUSES

ABILENE

Abilene, a fine house just off Newtownpark Avenue, was put up for sale in April 2018 with the expectation of raising €7 million.

The house, which has an area of just over 330m^2, is on just over a hectare of land. Substantial housing development is expected on the site.

The property dates back to 1790, when it was built as a farmhouse on the Proby estate; several outbuildings were added and the main house was extended in the 1950s. The house and its lands were bought in 1941 by Dermot Findlater, who ran the old Findlater shop chain, including one in Blackrock, for decades. He and his wife Elizabeth Dorothea had six children. Dermot died in 1962, but Elizabeth remained there for the rest of her life. She died in Abilene on 20 November 2017, just short of 108 years old, having been Ireland's oldest citizen for seventy-four days. In her will, she left €7,809,069.

Elizabeth Dorothea was the daughter of Captain Harry de Courcy-Wheeler, who accepted Pearse's surrender in 1916. She had a passion for golf, hockey and rugby, and married Dermot Findlater in 1932. The Findlater connection with Abilene lasted for seventy-seven years.

BLACKROCK HOUSE PRICES

Blackrock, along with Dalkey, has the highest number of property millionaires (people who own homes worth €1 million or more) in Ireland, according to a 2018 property survey conducted by the property website daft.ie. Nationwide, over 4,500 homes are worth €1 million or more and around 600 of these top-end houses are in the Blackrock area.

Since 2012, the salary required to get a mortage on a typical house in Blackrock has almost doubled, and currently stands at €165,857.

CROSS AVENUE HOUSING PLAN

One of the biggest current housing developments planned for Blackrock is on the site of Chesterfield House on Cross Avenue.

The house and its grounds, of just over 3 hectares, was once home to the late Tom Roche, who co-founded Roadstone, the building materials group, which is now known as CRH. Cairn Homes, which is also developing housing on part of the RTÉ campus in Donnybrook, acquired Chesterfield House and its lands in 2015, when it bought a loans portfolio from the Ulster Bank for close on €400 million. The original drawing room of Chesterfield House is a protected structure and can't be demolished, but the rest of it, added at later dates, as well as its derelict sheds, can be redeveloped.

Cairn Homes is planning to build 217 houses as well as apartments on the site.

HOUSE PRICES IN 2000

Blackrock house prices in 2000, nearly twenty years ago, were still way above average for the Dublin area.

The cheapest house price then was £190,000 for each of two cottages, both needing some renovation, at Annaville Avenue for Newtownpark Avenue. In contrast, a house sold on Waltham Terrace for just under £900,0000, while a Gothic style semi-detached house on South Hill Avenue went for £2.5 million. Even a house in poor condition, needing much renovation, on Idrone Terrace fetched £500,000. The Avoca Park development off Avoca Avenue, built in the early 1990s, was producing good resale prices nearly a decade later; one house, with four bedrooms, sold for £500,000. Estates off Carysfort Avenue were also producing good prices. A four-bedroom detached house on the Carysfort Downs estate went for close on £500,000.

The seaside view before the Covanta waste-to-energy incinerator at Poolbeg became operational and clearly visible from the seafront at Blackrock.

Apartments, too, were selling well in the Blackrock area in 2000, including Carysfort Hall, Castle Dawson on the main Rock Road, and Clonfadda Wood and The Elms on Mount Merrion Avenue. A two-bedroom ground floor apartment at Castle Dawson went for £275,000.

LAND AT NEWTOWNPARK HOUSE

Much of the land surrounding Newtownpark House was sold off between 1967 and 1972; Marian Court, Mount Albany, Pine Court, Richmond and Springfield were all built here, while a large section of the land, abutting on to the gardens of Newtownpark House, was kept as parkland, which still exists today.

MOUNT ALBANY SALE

A house sale at 68 Mount Albany, just off Newtownpark Avenue, in May 2018, astonished local residents with its low price (by Blackrock standards). The two-bedroom bungalow in a quiet, traffic-free cul-de-sac went on the market for €625,000.

PROBY PLACE

Proby Place, at the back of Proby Square, was once the one-hectare site owned by MacLysaght Nurseries, but in recent times, the site has been redeveloped for housing.

In May 2018, Glenveagh Properties was selling the first phase of its scheme of four- and five-bedroom semi-detached houses, twenty in all, each selling for around €1 million.

Planning permission had originally been given for this site in 2006 to O'Malley Homes, which planned to build twenty-seven three-storey terraced houses there. However, their plans aroused strong local objections.

TEMPLE ROAD EXPLOSION

Two houses on the main Temple Road were badly damaged by a gas explosion in 2009, although fortunately, no one was seriously injured. In 2015, Dún Laoghaire-Rathdown County Council announced plans to redevelop the site for social housing.

TEMPLE ROAD SITE

In the summer of 2017, a site of nearly four hectares just off Temple Road was put on the market for €25 million. It included a large period house and disused school buildings owned by the Daughters of Charity of St Vincent de Paul. The site is about 350m south-east of Blackrock village and 500m west of Seapoint DART station.

The lands have extensive frontage on to Temple Road and are bounded to the east by the St Vincent's Park residential scheme, to the west by the national office of the Alzheimer Society of Ireland (which was given its land by the Daughters of Charity) and to the south by Rockfield Park. St Teresa's House, which dates from 1862 and was originally known as Craigmore House, is due to be converted into upmarket apartments at the time of writing, while the development of the site is also expected to include just over 250 houses and

apartments. The new owner is expected to demolish a range of vacant school buildings dating mainly from the 1950s, which haven't been used since St Teresa's School closed in 1988 following its amalgamation with St Augustine's School in Obelisk Park in Blackrock. The gate lodge can't be developed as it is listed for preservation.

These lands were originally part of the wealthy Rockfield Estate, which was leased in 1862 to a wealthy wine and spirit merchant, Jonathan Hogg, who signed up to a ninety-nine-year lease. He built Craigmore House, which subsequently became St Teresa's House, and also sold 14 hectares to George Orr Wilson, who built the Italianate mansion of Dunardagh, now the provincial house of the Daughters of Charity of St Vincent de Paul.

Nuns from the Daughters of Charity bought Craigmore House in 1925, later renaming it St Teresa's House. For nearly a century, the nuns based in this convent provided services for people in need. These included a care home and school for orphaned boys, a residence and school for girls with intellectual disabilities, a similar home for adults, and a care facility and residential centre for people suffering from Alzheimer's. The order decided to use the money generated from the sale of all this land for its various ministries in Ireland and Kenya. In the decade before the sale, the order had provided £25 million to support various services for people with intellectual disabilities in the Dublin area.

8

NATURAL HISTORY

BLACKROCK PARK

The park is the largest open space in Blackrock, situated between the Rock Road and the railway line. The Rock Road itself is one of the oldest roads in Ireland, dating back about 2,000 years and originally built to link the Hill of Tara, where the High Kings of Ireland held court, and Co Wicklow.

Today, the park has extensive areas of greenery, as well as a picturesque pond with a small island where swans can be seen. The park also has a well-equipped children's playground.

Before the arrival of the Westland Row to Dunleary village railway line in 1834, people had access to a beach here, which was always very popular during the summer months. But after the railway line was built, the area between the beach and the railway line became flooded at high tide, creating very marshy conditions. It remained this way for years, until the Blackrock Town Commissioners, founded in 1860, decided to fill in the marshy area and create a park.

It took until the early 1870s for this to happen, however. In 1873, the Blackrock Town Commissioners took the bold step of borrowing £3,000 to build the park. When the park was being built, the granite gates at the entrance to the former Vauxhall House here were used to form the gated entrance to it, while what had been the gardens for Vauxhall House formed

the gardens close to the entrance to the park. In 2007, Dún Laoghaire-Rathdown county council published an extensive conservation and development plan for Blackrock Park, although it was never implemented. However, in 2016, the old bandstand in the park was refurbished.

The most recent outing of the local Teddy Bears' Picnic event was staged in Blackrock Park on 8 July 2018.

The present-day Blackrock Park, which remains a habitat for many seabirds, also has an unusual metal sculpture, close to Phoenix Terrace on the Williamstown side of the park. It is called Cut Out People and was created by Dan McCarthy and installed in 1986.

CARYSFORT COLLEGE GROUNDS

The grounds of the old Carysfort teacher training college in Blackrock were extensive, spreading to about 35 hectares, with large lawns, plenty of mature trees, and the Carysfort–Maretimo stream, the only one of its kind in Blackrock, which eventually discharges into Dublin Bay. It rises beyond Sandyford and runs for close on 8km. There are many bridges and culverts along its route, and after it has flowed through the Carysfort grounds, it then flows past Barclay Court on the Blackrock bypass.

What were the grounds of the old college have been well preserved by the present occupier of the site, UCD's Michael Smurfit Graduate Business School.

CARYSFORT PARK

This park is small, but well kept and tidy, off Carysfort Avenue. Its two main features are a children's playground and a small duck pond.

ROCKFIELD PARK

On lands that were once part of the estate of Newtownpark House, this park is just off Avondale Lawn extension. In addition to the park area, Rockfield Park also has two soccer pitches and a rugby pitch that is allocated to Newpark School rugby players.

TOBERNEA PARK

This small park, near the main road at Temple Hill, features a sculpture called Stele for Cecil King, made from mild steel plate by Colm Brennan, to commemorate one-time Blackrock resident and artist Cecil King. Nearby, off Tobernea Terrace, a holy well was once a popular pilgrimage site; the water from the well was believed to have been very efficacious in curing eye infections. People also took pieces of bark from the tree beside the well, and on that tree hung pieces of rag.

9

PUBS, RESTAURANTS AND LEISURE

AKASH INDIAN RESTAURANT

The Akash Indian restaurant at George's Avenue, just off the Main Street, first opened as a small family run restaurant in 1985. Since then, it has gone through various changes to the menus and the décor, all with the aim of providing the best possible Indian culinary experience.

BLUE ORCHID

The Blue Orchid opened at Newtownpark Avenue in 2002, serving Thai food. It has since become a firm favourite with diners from Blackrock and further afield.

CAFÉ JAVA

Café Java on Main Street in Blackrock offers a wide range of freshly ground coffees, together with speciality teas.

CONWAYS

For long a stalwart of the pub trade in Blackrock village, Conways was run for forty-four years by Liam Conway, after whom it is named. When he retired in 2002, he sold it to Dalkey publican John Roe for over €3.5 million. The present-day pub, which has frontages to both Main Street and George's Avenue, serves food all day and evening and also has a wide selection of craft beers.

CUP AND COIN CAFÉ

This modest but enticing café is one of the highlights at Blackrock Market, just off Main Street.

THE DARK HORSE

The Dark Horse, which was owned by the Galway Bay brewery group until 2017, is based in Carysfort Avenue, where it claims to have the best selection in south Dublin of craft and small batch beers from around the world. The pub also has a beer garden in front and an off licence section. Before it was transformed into The Dark Horse, it used to be the Avoca, a modest and unpretentious family pub.

In the 1980s, McGowan's off licence and deli was next door to the Avoca lounge. In the 1960s, the Shields pub was located here. Going even further back, to the 1940s, the premises were occupied by Joseph Searson's grocery and wine shop. In the 1980s, another pub was located close by, at No. 39 Carysfort Avenue, with the curious title of the U Inn.

EDDIE ROCKET'S

The Blackrock branch of Eddie Rocket's, in Main Street, is part of a nationwide chain offering a tempting array of fast food dishes.

ENCORE CAFÉ

Based in the Blackrock shopping centre, Encore Café offers plenty of coffee and lunch treats.

FELLINI'S

Fellini's, at Deansgrange Road, offers a tempting selection of home-made pizzas, pasta and desserts.

FLASH HARRY'S

Flash Harry's, on Temple Road, serves a wide selection of food, as well as cocktails, wines and other drinks.

GLORY CHINESE RESTAURANT

The Glory Chinese restaurant on Main Street in Blackrock is as noted for its striking design, with its deep red walls and Chinese vases, as it is for its cuisine. A forerunner in Chinese cuisine in Blackrock was the Great Wall takeaway, near the old post office. The present-day Great Wall is beside the A-Roy Thai takeaway on the Temple Road, close to the heart of Blackrock village. This was once the site of the Prontaprint branch in Blackrock, set up in the mid-1980s. The old Great Wall takeaway used to be on Main Street, close to the former post office building, in the 1970s.

HERON & GREY

The Heron & Grey restaurant at 19A Main Street, which had one Michelin star took over from the Canteen restaurant in 2015 and had a reputation far beyond Blackrock for its modern, intensely flavoured, international cuisine, created with seasonal ingredients, and full of contrasting textures and tastes. However, its seating capacity was limited, meaning that would-be diners there had to book months in advance. It seated fewer than twenty customers at a time and didn't even have a lavatory, but that didn't prevent it becoming a gastronomic sensation. It was fairly expensive; in the spring of 2018, it was promoting a tasting menu for €74.

Andrew Heron managed front of house and Damien Grey was the head chef. According to the ViaMichelin website, Heron & Grey, one of the smallest Michelin-starred restaurants in the world, served lunch on Fridays and Saturdays, and dinners from Thursday to Saturday. There were two seatings

for dinner, at 7.30 p.m. and 8.30 p.m.The five-course dinner menu changed every two weeks, according to ViaMichelin, which described the restaurant as 'homely and candlelit'.

In 2018 it was announced that Heron would be leaving the business in the New Year, and co-owner Damien Grey was planning to open a new restaurant using the same premises, in March 2019. Called *Liath*, the restaurant will specialise in new Irish cuisine.

JACK O'ROURKES

This pub on Main Street dates back to 1897, although there has been a tavern on the site since the mid-eighteenth century. O'Rourke's and the Three Tun pub nearby are the oldest surviving pubs in the district.

O'Rourke's interior features many fascinating old photographs of the famous and infamous people who have frequented it over the years. The better known ones include-James Joyce, Myles na gCopaleen and Seán O'Sullivan, the painter. While most of the present-day pub was built in 1897, a date engraved on the facade, it didn't become O'Rourke's until 1921, when Mary O'Rourke took over the premises. In those days, it wasn't just a pub, but also a grocery shop and a tea merchant.

One of her sons, Jack O'Rourke, took over the running of the pub in the 1930s and managed it until his retirement in 1977. Today, the fourth generation of O'Rourkes are minding this venerable hostelry.

KENZ

This intriguing restaurant on Blackrock's Main Street offers a wide selection of Moroccan-style dishes, cooked in the home style.

LAZY DAYS CAFÉ

Lazy Days is a little off the beaten track, at Sydney Terrace, which provides an oasis of calm after the hustle and bustle of Main Street. It offers a wide range of coffees together with paninis.

LIDO CAFÉ

The Lido Café was a well-known institution in Blackrock in the 1940s, located at 11 Main Street and owned and run by Thomas Murphy.

MELLOW FIG

One of Blackrock's newest restaurants, Mellow Fig is based at George's Avenue, just off Main Street near Le Pastis bistro.

MELON FAIR

In the late-eighteenth century, a curious annual event was held in Conway's tavern, then one of two pubs in Blackrock. The annual feast celebrated melons, of which a considerable number were put on display in Conway's. A newspaper report in August 1787 recorded that the annual melon festival that year had attracted around 200 people to the pub, all of whom enjoyed the many melons on offer. At that time, the only other pub in Blackrock was the Three Tun Tavern, which is still trading today.

BREFFNI LOUNGE

This is a traditional, family-run pub on the Main Street, sometimes described as a cosy old men's pub.

OLD PUBS

The Blackrock district had quite a number of pubs and wine shops that failed to survive to the present day. In the 1960s, Patrick Guilfoyle ran a wine and spirits shop at 39 Main Street, which by the early 1970s had been transformed into the Frascati Inn, run by Michael Mullen, while the Newtownpark Avenue area district had Colgan's bar and lounge, owned and run by John Colgan.

OUZOS BAR AND GRILL

This bar and grill opened in 2010, serving steaks and seafood on the site of the old Mad Hatter pub on Main Street in Blackrock.

PARK RESTAURANT

The old Park Restaurant, run by celebrated chef Colin O'Daly, thrived in Blackrock in the 1980s, close to where the Bank of Ireland branch is now located on Main Street. Although the restaurant didn't last, in many ways it was progenitor of Roly's Bistro, which is still going strong in Ballsbridge after thirty years.

THE PLAYWRIGHT

The old Playwright pub used to be a popular destination at the corner of Newtownpark Avenue and Newtown Park; it was on the site of the old Colgan's pub, which traded in the 1970s. The Playwright was sold in 2004 for €8.1 million to an unidentified buyer. Subsequently, it was turned into a branch of TGI Fridays. Among its more recent owners was Arthur Ryan, the man who turned Penneys/Primark into such an international success.

The Playwright was often described as a 'pub for all people'. During the day and into the evening, it offered a full 'pub grub' menu, while on Saturday evenings, it held music sessions upstairs for younger people. The lounge remained a pleasant place for a quiet pint. The pub has been closed for nearly a decade now.

Ciaran and Colum Butler, who have the Starbucks franchise for Ireland, bought the Playwright in 2014 and obtained planning permission to turn it into a shop. Since then, there have been many rumours that Aldi or Lidl was going to take over the site, but that never materialised. Then, in August 2018, it was announced that Dunnes Stores was planning to turn it into an upmarket food store. At the time of writing this conversion is in progress, and the new shop is set to open shortly.

RAGE

This is one of the most recently opened restaurants in Blackrock, at 65 Main Street, serving flame-grilled food and a great casual dining experience, as well as many wines and craft beers.

SIGN OF THE SHIP

This old tavern in Blackrock flourished in the mid-eighteenth century, when it was owned and run by Thomas Gambell and his wife, Hannah Peters, the daughter of a landscape gardener called Mathew Peters and his wife Elizabeth Younge. Hannah was born in about 1740 on the Isle of Wight, where her father was working at the time. She came to Dublin as a young girl, and her father set up a seed and gardening shop close to the Hammond Lane foundry near the northern banks of the River Liffey.

Thomas Gambell and Hannah Peters married in Dublin in 1761. Their pub was based near Tobernea Terrace, overlooking Dublin Bay and not far from the present day DART station at Seapoint. In its heyday, it was the main pub in the area and even had its own ballroom. It also had an alternative name, the Man o' War.

Hannah Peters was widowed in 1769 but she continued running the pub, which became known as the Widow

Gambell's. She sold the pub in 1775 to a Londoner, Augustine Moore, who changed it to the then-popular style of pubs in London. He put less emphasis on food and entertainment and more on a wide range of wines and other alcoholic beverages. No records survive of what happened to Hannah Peters after she sold the pub and her other assets in 1775. Neither did the Sign of the Ship tavern survive; all trace of it is long vanished.

STARBUCKS

Starbucks was based in the old post office building on Main Street, one of several businesses there. However, the post office building was sold in 2014 and is now awaiting redvelopment, while Starbucks has moved a short distance away, still on Main Street.

3 LEAVES

The 3 Leaves Indian restaurant in Blackrock Market has been operating for over three years now, and has built up an excellent reputation for its cuisine. Its prices are very reasonable, with a €10 charge for lunch. The name of this small restaurant comes from coriander, mint and curry leaves.

THREE TUN TAVERN

These licensed premises were once three separate properties: 1, 3 and 5 Temple Road, which over the years accommodated a number of different businesses. The middle property housed a cycle fitters and agent for some seventy years, while the property at the corner of Temple Road and Carysfort Avenue became a pub in the 1950s. In the 1980s, it was renamed Cary's Fort Bar. The history of the Three Tun tavern here can be traced back to the late eighteenth century, when it was owned by a bishop and said to have been a place of good cheer.

The latest phase in the history of the Three Tun Tavern came when the premises were taken over by the English pub chain J.D. Wetherspoon. After a major refurbishment job, the pub was reopened in July 2014.

THE WICKED WOLF

Based at No. 2 Main Street, Blackrock, this is a loud and lively venue that is especially popular with a younger crowd. The food it serves is secondary to dancing, music and a general late-night good time.

WISHING WELL

The Wishing Well pub in Newtown Park is said to derive its name from an ancient wishing well that once stood on the site. The pub serves food seven days a week and is noted as a venue for all sporting occasions. It also has a beer garden and, unlike its once near neighbour the Playwright, it is thriving.

WOODEN SPOON

Described, with perfect accuracy, as a 'cute takeaway and deli', the Wooden Spoon is at Bath Place in Blackrock, just off Main Street on the way to Blackrock railway station. It offers breakfast, brunch and lunch.

10

REMARKABLE PEOPLE

RICHARD BOYD BARRETT

Richard Boyd Barrett is a People Before Profit TD who has been in the Dáil for the Dún Laoghaire constituency since the 2011 general election. He was first elected to the local county council in 2009 and then to the Dáil two years later, after nine years of trying. Ever since, he has been one of the most interesting and most controversial politicians at national level.

In terms of international politics, Boyd Barrett is chair of the Irish Anti-War movement and in 2003, helped organise mass protests against the war in Iraq, while he has also been a consistent supporter of Palestinian rights. In Ireland he has consistently railed against establishment politics and has been very critical of many national initiatives, such as the setting up of the National Asset Management Agency (NAMA). In the Dún Laoghaire constituency, he has long been vehement about many local development issues.

Boyd Barrett's birth mother is the actor Sinéad Cusack, with whom he was later reunited. In 2013, he claimed that his biological father was theatre director Vincent Dowling. He was raised by his adoptive parents in Glenageary: David Boyd Barrett, an accountant, and his wife Valerie.

MARY BYRNE

Mary Byrne and another Blackrock resident, Frances Dillon, were two of the wealthiest landowners who have ever lived in the Blackrock area. In 1876, the two women were recorded as owning an astonishing amount of land in Co Donegal – nearly 1,400 hectares.

PATRICK BYRNE

Patrick Byrne, who lived from 1783 until 1864, spent the last nine years of his life at 3 Waltham Terrace in Blackrock. He was well known in Dublin as an ecclesiastical architect and one of his designs was for the Church of St John the Baptist in Blackrock. He was also a vice-president of the Royal Institute of Architects of Ireland.

DR JOHN COLOHAN

Dr John Colohan was a medical practitioner who lived in Blackrock and was renowned for owning the first motor car in Ireland.

In 1898, he bought a Benz Velo, which created a minor sensation in and around Blackrock as the avant garde motorist drove around in his open-topped car. The vehicle was featured in a 1989 stamp series devoted to Irish motor classics. In 1985, it was purchased by Denis Dowdall of Irish Motor Distributors, who had it restored to full working order.

Dr Colohan was clearly devoted to the new art of motoring and by 1902 he also owned a Daimler, described at the time as the smartest car in Dublin. But while he sustained his addiction to fast, top-range cars, he didn't sustain his medical connections. In 1910, he bought the Grand Hotel in Malahide, north Co Dublin, for £10,000, and for most of the rest of his life he was a hotelier rather than a doctor.

LIAM DEVALLY

Liam Devally (1933–2018) had a very varied career, firstly as a singer, quiz show host and broadcaster, and later making a complete about-turn in middle age to become a barrister and then a circuit court judge. He and his family lived for many years in Blackrock.

Devally was born in Cahir, Co Tipperary, where his father was a Garda, but later the family moved to Mullingar when his father was transferred there. Liam was educated at St Enda's College, Galway, where he became fluent in Irish. He soon enjoyed considerable success as a boy soprano, winning a gold medal at the 1947 Feis Ceoil. Later, the composer Seán Ó Riada wrote a number of songs in Irish for him. Liam went on to perform extensively in Canada and the US with the Irish Festival Singers.

Devally had also joined Radio Éireann, now RTÉ, in 1953, becoming one of the station's youngest continuity announcers. Moving into light entertainment after the Irish television service had started in 1962, he was the quiz master on Cross Country Quiz from 1969 until 1973, with questions set by Peter Murphy. Liam also co-presented an Irish music and dance show with Kathleen Watkins, wife of Gay Byrne.

When Devally was 23, he married Mairéad, who was more senior than him at RTÉ, and they settled in Blackrock, where they lived for the rest of their lives.

In the mid-1970s, while still working at RTÉ, Devally started studying to become a barrister. Eventually, in 1991, he was appointed a circuit court judge. Following his retirement, he was often to be seen walking in Blackrock or pushing Mairéad in her wheelchair. Mairéad predeceased Liam, who died in April 2018 at the age of 85 and is survived by his children, Mary and Conor. After the funeral at St John the Baptist's church in Blackrock, Devally was buried at Kilmacanogue cemetery in north Co Wicklow.

JOHN BOYD DUNLOP

John Boyd Dunlop (1840–1921) developed the first practical pneumatic tyre for cars and was one of the founders of the rubber tyre company that bears his name. For some of his adult life, he lived in a big eighteenth-century house in the Blackrock area called South Hill.

MICHAEL FARRELL

Michael Farrell (1899–1962) spent much of his adult life writing an acclaimed novel – his only one – called *Thy Tears Might Cease.*

He was born in Carlow, where his parents owned a hardware store, before the family moved to Dublin in 1924. The young Farrell had some extraordinary adventures and misadventures. He started to study medicine at UCD, but was then imprisoned for six months during the civil war. When he was let out, he did a walking tour of Europe with a fellow medical student and then went to work in the marine customs' service in what was then the Belgian Congo. He returned home to his medical studies, this time at Trinity, but soon gave them up to work in journalism.

Farrell worked for Radio Éireann for several years and was also a frequent contributor to *The Bell*, Sean O'Faolain's literary magazine. In 1937, the epic *Thy Tears Might Cease* was accepted by a publisher in London at the behest of O'Faolain. Farrell spent the next fifteen years trying to edit it and cut down the vast length of the text; in the end, his good friend Monk Gibbon reduced it by 100,000 words. The novel was finally published in 1963 and became an international bestseller, translated into many languages. By the time it came out, Farrell had been dead a year.

In 1930, Farrell married Frances Cahill, who ran the Crock of Gold hand-weaving business. After Farrell gave up journalism, he moved into the management of his wife's business. In 1943, the Farrells bought St Ita's on Newtownpark Avenue in Blackrock. It had been the Glebe house for the Church of Ireland parish of Stillorgan and Kilmacud from 1764 until 1882, and the Farrells bought the house and the land from John D. Valentine, who had run a dairy farm there since 1920. They brought with them the Crock of Gold business, which they set up in Newtownpark Avenue. It produced superb hand-woven tweed in soft shades reminiscent of the Irish countryside. A quarter of a century after Farrell died, however, the business got into difficulties and in 1989 it closed down – a great loss to the Blackrock district.

TONY FARRELL

Tony Farrell ran a well-known bakery in Blackrock for many years and was noted for his many other generous contributions to Irish life, including sport.

He studied at Castleknock College, where he had many family links, and then went on to study bakery technology at the Polytechnic of the South Bank in London. For many years subsequently, he was the managing director of O'Leary's Bakeries at the top of Sweetman's Avenue in Blackrock. For a long time it was the only pitta bread bakery in Ireland and was renowned far and wide in the catering trade for its bread rolls. Farrell had much involvement with organisations and events for the bakery trade and was renowned for his generosity.

Farrell was closely connected all his life with athletics, and became president of Donore Harriers. He was also a patron of the arts, closely involved with the United Arts Club in Upper Fitzwilliam Street, Dublin. Married, with five children, he was heartbroken by the untimely death of his daughter, Helen, who died on 5 September 2001. Very sadly, less than a year later, on 15 June 2002, Tony Farrell died when a routine medical examination went wrong. He was survived by his wife Yvonne and four children, Hugh, Jane, Lia and Tim.

DR JOHN FLEETWOOD

Dr John Fleetwood (1917–2007) was a well-known GP in Blackrock for many years, and was also in the public eye as a regular contributor to the *Sunday Miscellany* programme on RTÉ Radio 1.

He was born into a noted medical family in Edinburgh, but they moved to Plymouth and then to Bray, Co Wicklow, in his early teens. Fleetwood studied at Presentation College, Bray, then Blackrock College, going on to study medicine at UCD. During the Second World War, he was assistant master at the Coombe Women and Infants University Hospital in Dublin.

After the war, he worked for Dr O'Grady's medical practice in Donnybrook, before setting up his own practice at Proby Square in Blackrock in 1947, which became the Carysfort Clinic.

In those early days, if he found himself on call close to the Forty Foot in Sandycove, and if he was accompanied by a medical student – who were nearly all male at that time – he would often suggest taking time out for a 'dip in the nip'.

Fleetwood always had a keen interest in the welfare of the elderly and in 1961, he was appointed to Our Lady's Hospice in Blackrock.

Fleetwood's son John, one of his four children, joined his father's practice in 1978 and is still running it today.

During his time at UCD, Dr Fleetwood also discovered a parallel career: radio broadcasting. He was invited to compere a programme on a UCD rag week that was being broadcast on Radio Éireann, and he enjoyed it so much that he continued broadcasting for the rest of his life. He also had a great sense of humour and put this to great use on one piece for *Sunday Miscellany* when he described a family holiday in northern France. The plumbing system went badly wrong and the local 'expert' on the subject turned out to be anything but. When he finished his work and turned the system back on again, it all blew up and, as Fleetwood described it, most of the downstairs of the house was liberally coated with 'merde'. The 'expert' was called Jean-Paul Sartre, another source of amusement for Fleetwood.

Apart from his radio work, Fleetwood also often appeared on *The Late Late Show* on television, where he frequently demonstrated the Heimlich manoeuvre to clear the airways of a person who was choking. He also wrote extensively, including a history of medicine in Ireland in 1951, and a volume on Irish body snatchers in 1988. He also researched the life of

Thomas Proby (1665–1729), a local landowner after whom Proby Square in Blackrock is named.

Fleetwood and his wife of fifty-five years, Ann O'Connor, who predeceased him, also travelled a great deal. They traversed the length and breadth of the Soviet Union in 1961, at a time when few people ventured there. During that trip, Fleetwood shot vast amounts of 8mm colour film, so much in fact that years later, RTÉ was able to make a whole television programme out of it.

ROWAN GILLESPIE

Rowan Gillespie, born in Blackrock in 1953, is a well-known sculptor whose studio is in his native Blackrock.

Gillespie's father, Jack, was a medical doctor, while his mother, Moira, was a judge in the Supreme Court. When he was young, his family lived in Cyprus and Rowan was sent to boarding school in England. When he was 16, he enrolled at York School of Art in the north of England, which is where he was first introduced to the lost wax casting process and where he met Hanne, who became his wife. She now runs the Clonlea yoga studio in Blackrock.

From York, the young Gillespie went to Kingston College of Art, also in England, and then proceeded to the Statens Kunstole in Oslo. In Norway, he also lectured for three years at the Munch museum and has subsequently said that Munch has had the greatest artistic influence on him, right up to the present day. He and Hanne married in 1974 and that same year, he had his first solo exhibition in Norway. The couple returned to live in Dublin in 1977, when he set up his foundry and workshop in Blackrock. Over the next twenty years, he had several solo exhibitions at the Solomon Gallery in Dublin, while he also took part in many group shows throughout Europe and the US.

Subsequently, Gillespie decided to concentrate on site-specific sculpture, producing such works as the Famine sculpture on Custom House Quay in Dublin and a series of statues on a similar theme in Toronto. One of his most recent works has been the Proclamation group outside Kilmainham Gaol in Dublin. In his native Blackrock, his creation the Blackrock Dolmen stands beside Main Street, close to St John the Baptist Catholic church. He also created a striking sculpture of Sir William Orpen, the locally born man who became a renowned society painter in the early twentieth century. This sculpture was originally destined for the shopping centre in Stillorgan but has now been transferred to the front of the Talbot Hotel on the main N11 road at Stillorgan.

REGINALD GRAY

Reginald Gray (1930–2013), had a very conventional upbringing in Blackrock, and blossomed into a highly skilled but unconventional artist, who spent the last fifty years of his life in France, mostly in Paris.

Gray grew up on Avoca Avenue; his father worked for Guinness. Reginald was educated at All Saints Church of Ireland national school in Carysfort Avenue before going on to the old Blackrock Technical Institute and then to the National College of Art & Design in Dublin for a brief period. Most of his art education came from the tuition provided by Cecil Ffrench Salkeld, whose daughter, Beatrice, married Brendan Behan in 1955. Gray had become very friendly with Behan at that stage and was his best man at their 7.30 am wedding in the Church of the Sacred Heart in Donnybrook, although some have disputed that he was ever there and claim that the Sacristan was the best man.

In the early 1950s, he set up his own studio in Lower Leeson Street before becoming very involved with the nearby Pike Theatre, as its designer. He designed the sets for its production of *The Rose Tattoo* by Tennessee Williams in 1957, which caused huge controversy because it suggested during a performance that a condom had been dropped on the stage.

By then, Gray had tired of the narrow cliques who made up artistic life in Dublin, and that year, 1957, he moved to what he saw as wider freedoms in London, where one of his famous portraits was that of Dublin-born artist Francis Bacon, completed in 1960. He didn't spend long in London, however, and in 1963, as his marriage was breaking down, he moved to France. For his first year there, Gray lived in Rouen, where he started off as a pavement artist and gained a lot of work as an extra in local opera productions. Then he moved to

Paris, where he remained for the rest of his life, apart from a ten-year spell when he lived in a chateau 80km north of the city. In Paris, Gray had a number of other jobs apart from being a portrait painter. He also worked as a sub-editor for the *International Herald Tribune*, and as a photographer and cameraman filming the Paris fashion collections.

It is as a portrait painter that Gray made his reputation, however, painting such writers as Samuel Beckett, Brendan Behan and Harold Pinter, as well as stars of the fashion world such as Yves St Laurent. His works are in many museums and art galleries, including the Dublin Writers' Museum and the National Portrait Gallery in London. After a very fruitful life as a painter, he died in his adopted city, Paris, in 2013, aged 82, and was survived by his three children and his second partner, Doina.

MARY HANAFIN

Born in Thurles, Co Tipperary, Mary Hanafin's father was the late senator, Des Hanafin. Before getting involved in politics, she worked as a teacher of Irish and History at the Dominican College at Sion Hill in Blackrock.

She married Eamon Leahy, a senior counsel, in 1985, but, he died suddenly in 2003 aged 46. The couple had no children.

As for her entry into politics, Hanafin got into the Dáil in 1997, on her second attempt, becoming a TD for the Dún Laoghaire constituency. In 2002, she gained her first ministerial role when she was appointed Minister of State for Children. Within a couple of years, she had been made government chief whip, the first woman to hold that position. Between 2004 and 2011, she held a total of four ministerial positions, until she lost her seat at the 2011 general election to Richard Boyd Barrett.

In the 2016 general election, she failed to gain a seat in the Dáil, but had become a councillor for the Blackrock area in 2014 and remains one today. She also continues to be an often divisive figure due to her role in several controversies and political spats.

Hanafin's fellow councillors in Blackrock are Marie Baker (FG), Anne Colgan (Independent), Kate Feeney (FF), Deirdre Kingston (Labour) and Barry Ward (FG).

SARAH MAUD HECKFORD

Sarah Maud Heckford was born in Blackrock as Sarah Maud Goff, and her father was a banker. As a young child, she developed TB and although she recovered from it, the disease had permanent effects on her posture and gait.

Despite this, Heckford had a full life, mostly outside Ireland. In the late 1860s, she was a co-founder with her husband Nathaniel of the East London Hospital for Children and Dispensary for Women. Later she moved to India, then to South Africa. Her first book was entitled *The Life of Christ and its Bearing on the Doctrines of Communism*, published in 1873. She also wrote a number of travel books, including one about her time in the Transvaal, published in 1882. She died in Pretoria in 1903, aged 63.

EDDIE HERON

Eddie Heron, a noted swimmer, was one of the best-known sporting personalities connected with Blackrock.

He was born in Dublin in 1910 and became a keen swimmer as a young man; he had a particular reputation as a diver.

He first came to prominence at the Tailteann Games in 1924 and went on make many more appearances at the Blackrock Baths. Heron made many dives into the swimming baths at Blackrock, and its diving structure was built for him. He went on to represent Ireland at swimming in the London Olympics in 1948. After he died in 1985, a plaque in his honour was put up at the railway station in Blackrock.

JOHNNY ON THE ROCK ROAD

In the late 1970s and early 1980s, a well-known figure in Blackrock was a homeless man called simply Johnny. He was dressed in a bizarre mixture of outfits and had a long, black beard. Some people in the area compared him to the Messiah and it seemed as if he believed this himself, as he walked to and fro along the Rock Road every day, with a long wooden pole on his shoulder.

Johnny had no fixed abode and people in Blackrock were unsure where he actually spent his nights when he wasn't carrying his pole, or how he managed to scrounge enough to keep himself going. He became almost part of the street furniture on Rock Road, although no one knew who he was or why he was homeless. Then, suddenly, people noticed that he had simply vanished, never to reappear.

JAMES JOYCE

The well-known writer James Joyce (1882–1941) lived at many different locations in Dublin with his family in his younger days – a grand total of twenty-three different addresses before he and his wife, Nora Barnacle, emigrated to mainland Europe, living first in Zurich, then Trieste, before spending much of the 1920s and '30s in Paris. His final destination was Zurich, where he died in 1941.

One of the many places his family lived when Joyce was a young boy was at Leoville, 23 Carysfort Avenue in Blackrock, where they were in residence from late November 1891 until the early days of 1892. They moved house so often because of his father's financial difficulties. Joyce was 9 at the time he lived in Blackrock.

FRANK KELLY

Frank Kelly (1938–2016) was a long-time actor who found immense fame, if not fortune, towards the end of his life when he was one of the stars of the *Father Ted* series, which first aired on Channel 4.

Kelly was born in Blackrock on 28 December 1938, and within a few days was brought to the family home on Mount Merrion Avenue. For the rest of his life, he lived solely in Blackrock, apart from a spell in Monkstown after he got married. Born Francis O'Kelly, his name was shortened to Frank Kelly when he began acting. As a young man, he graduated from UCD with a Bachelor of Law degree, and although he went on to be called to the Bar, he never practised. He married Bairbre Nealon in 1964 and they remained married until his death. They had seven children together.

In December, 1983, Kelly had a hit in the UK Top 30 with his *Christmas Countdown* record, which was a spoof on *The Twelve Days of Christmas*. It reached number twenty-six in the UK singles chart and Kelly even had a letter from the Queen, telling him that the record had given her much pleasure.

While he was always in work as an actor, real fame eluded Kelly until the *Father Ted* series started in 1995 and he was cast as the literally filthy and foul-mouthed Father Jack. He later revealed that for every appearance as this obnoxious character, it took two hours for him to be made up. He said that if he was in costume, none of the other members of the cast would sit beside him, and he didn't blame them. He had Vaseline coming out of his ears to simulate a discharge, incontinence stains on his trousers, prosthetic teeth (which he took out so that he could eat) and a 'blind' eye created by an opaque lens.

After his appearances in *Father Ted*, Kelly's acting career on television and in films blossomed. He died on the eighteenth anniversary of the death of Dermot Morgan, who played Father Ted. Morgan died on Sunday 28 February 1998 and Kelly died on Sunday 28 February 2016.

CHARLES KICKHAM

Charles Kickham (1828–82) was a novelist and poet as well as a journalist, and he was one of the most prominent members of the Irish Republican Brotherhood. He lived at 2 Montpelier Place, off Temple Road.

CECIL KING

Cecil King (1921–86) developed a great reputation as an abstract/minimalist painter.

Born in Rathdrum, Co Wicklow, he was almost entirely self-taught as a painter. He had his first one-man show in 1959 despite still working full-time as a businessman, not devoting all his time to his artistic career until 1964. For many years, he lived and worked at Idrone Terrace in Blackrock.

HUGH LAMBERT

Hugh Lambert (1944–2005) was a well-known personality in the newspaper business in Dublin.

He joined the *Evening Press* and the *Sunday Press* in 1962 as a sub-editor, then from 1971 until 1980 he was the film critic for the *Sunday Press*, moving on to become production editor of that newspaper. In 1987, he was made editor of the *Irish Press*, which in a failed attempt to stop its stalling circulation, switched from broadsheet to tabloid. It lasted until 1995, when the *Irish Press* group closed down. The following year, Lambert was very involved in the launch of a new Dublin evening newspaper, the *Evening News*, which only lasted four months. He spent the last years of his career working with *The Irish Times*.

Although Lambert was resident in Glenageary with his wife and children, he died at the end of December 2005, in Blackrock Hospice on Sweetman's Avenue. He had returned from a trip to the US three months previously, apparently in good health, but on his return to Dublin developed a terminal illness.

FRED LEE

Fred Lee (1920–2016) was a colourful business figure who for many years ran a packaging company at Brookfield Terrace in Blackrock.

He was brought up in India, where his father Norman managed a coffee plantation, but his father died young in 1932 as a result of illnesses from his time in the trenches during the First World War. The Lee family ended up back in Dublin, in dire financial straits. Lee's mother, Frances, took all kinds of jobs, from pianist at silent movies to managing a hotel at Castletownbere in West Cork. Lee finished his schooling in very poor circumstances at a charity school near London for the sons of First World War victims.

During the Second World War, Lee served in the Royal Navy and after the war, he returned to Dublin, where in 1947, he bought out a bankrupt firm that made packaging and renamed it Industrial Packaging. The firm started in Harmony Row, Dublin, then moved to much larger premises in Blackrock. His immediate commercial neighbour there was a trade publishing firm that had started in rooms next to the old post office in Blackrock in 1970. Like so many other publishing companies, however, that firm failed to realise the threat posed by the arrival of the internet, and went bust a decade ago. Lee's packaging firm thrived, however, and it quadrupled its space by moving to a factory on the outskirts of Bray. Today, Industrial Packaging is the largest supplier of fibre drums and cardboard tubes in Ireland. The company is now run by some of Lee's sons. The former premises of the company in Brookfield Avenue, Blackrock, is now occupied by Blackrock Providers, builders' merchants.

The colourful and individualistic Fred Lee lived with his wife Pat and their family in Cabinteely for many years, but he ended up in a nursing home in Bray. He died there in November 2016, in the presence of his daughter, at the age of 97. Characteristically, he was laid to rest in Redford cemetery, Greystones, in a very unusual way – buried not in a coffin, but in a 65cm diameter cardboard tube normally used for casting concrete columns.

HARRY LYSTER

Lieutenant General Harry Lyster (1830–1922) was born in Blackrock into a leading Anglo–Irish family. During his military career with the British Army, he was awarded the Victoria Cross.

DR EDWARD MACLYSAGHT

Dr Edward MacLysaght (1887–1986) was renowned for his expertise in the field of genealogy. This historian of families was appointed Chief Herald and main genealogical officer in 1943, and was long regarded as an expert on families, both noble and humble, throughout Ireland. In many ways, he fuelled the vast public interest in genealogy that is so evident today.

MacLysaght lived for many years on Newtownpark Avenue in Blackrock, where he maintained a market garden. His property was just behind the Church of the Guardian Angels, which opened in 1968. The business that he set up in 1938, MacLysaght and Company, is still going today, with two of his descendants – Brian MacLysaght and Robert Anthony MacLysaght – the directors. Growing and selling a variety of plants, the company specialises in horticulture and is a wholesale supplier of nursery products.

As for Edward MacLysaght himself, he had an extraordinary life. He was born in a small village near Bristol called Flax Bourton. His father, Sidney, came from Cork, while his mother, although from Lincolnshire, was of Irish extraction. He was educated at Bristol, then at Rugby School, before going up to Corpus Christi College in Oxford to study law. His time there only lasted two terms, however.

MacLysaght injured himself whilst playing in a rugby match, and that injury changed his life. He was sent to Lahinch in Co Clare to recuperate, and spent six months living in a caravan. While he was there, he met several MacLysaghts and developed a strong affinity with his father's side of the family. Although he was born Lysaght, he added 'Mac' at this stage in his life. While he was living in Co Clare, he also developed a great interest in Irish history and by talking with many local people soon acquired a good knowledge of the Irish language.

When MacLysaght was 23, his father bought for him a farm of nearly 250 hectares, at Raheen in Co Clare. The young man soon installed a generator to provide electric light, forty years before rural electrification. He also developed a school, where young men could learn about the mechanics of farming.

The young MacLysaght was also deeply involved in the Irish cultural revival. At its height, in 1913, he married Mabel Pattison. By 1915, his Irish had improved so much that he founded a Neo-Gaeltacht Irish language community in Raheen. He was also a co-founder of the Maunsel Press.

MacLysaght also became very involved politically, vehemently opposing John Redmond's compromises on home rule for Ireland at the 1917/18 Irish Convention. It is not known if he was a member of the Old IRA, but he certainly gave financial and other support to the East Clare brigade of the organisation, led by Michael and Conn Brennan. MacLysaght's office in Raheen was also used as a meeting place for members of the local IRA, and guns, ammunition and documents were stored there. The war of independence led to a sharp decline in the farm's fortunes, however, not helped by subsequent frequent British Army raids and the execution of some of his close Republican friends.

MacLysaght became a loyal supporter of the new TD for Co Clare, Éamon de Valera. After he returned from Britain, however, where he had been part of a Sinn Féin delegation that was publicising the Black and Tan atrocities in Ireland, MacLysaght was thrown into prison.

His fortunes changed with the setting up of the new Free State in 1922, when he was elected to the new Seanad. He began his long career writing about family history, building on the work of Rev Patrick Woulfe, whose book *Irish Names and Surnames*, published in 1923, paved the way for much genealogical work. MacLysaght stayed in the Seanad until 1925 and later, in 1929, he made the first of four trips to South Africa as a journalist, later writing up his experiences there in Irish.

By the end of the 1930s, Maclysaght had been made an inspector of the Irish Manuscripts Commission and later, from 1956 until 1973, he chaired the commission. In 1942, he was elected to the Royal Irish Academy and that same year was appointed to the governing body of the School of Celtic Studies. Then in 1943 came a key appointment, when de Valera made MacLysaght the Chief Herald, a job he held until 1954. He was in charge of the state's genealogical resources and was also the Keeper of Manuscripts in the National Library of Ireland from 1948 until 1954. He also continued to publish extensively, right up to the early 1980s.

MacLysaght wrote his memoirs towards the end of his life, but when he offered them to a publisher in London they declined them, saying that while the publishing house could withstand one libel action, it wouldn't be able to survive forty.

Edward MacLysaght moved to Blackrock in the early 1930s and after he set up a nursery business at Upper Proby Square, he continued to have an extraordinary dual career as an academic and genealogist as well as the owner of a thriving company. He died in Blackrock on 4 March 1986.

MYLES MCWEENEY

Myles McWeeney, a well-known Dublin journalist, was once a familiar figure in Blackrock, where he lived for a number of years at 47 Carysfort Avenue.

McWeeney comes from a family with a long pedigree of journalism, going back to the days of the *Freeman's Journal*, on which one of his ancestors was the chief reporter, equivalent to editor. Myles worked on *The Late Late Show* on RTÉ for seven years and went on to work for the *Irish Independent* for a further twenty-five years, where he ended up specialising in writing about food and wine. He took voluntary redundancy from that newspaper in 2007 and moved on to write about the same topics for *Social & Personal* magazine.

Myles married Laurie Carr, then working for RTÉ, in 1995; she is now the general manager of Great Music in Irish Houses. In recent years, they have lived – and continue to live – in Sandymount.

MARY MITCHELL-O'CONNOR

A TD for the Dún Laoghaire constituency, Mary Mitchell-O'Connor has a constituency office in Blackrock.

Born in 1957, she worked as a teacher until she entered the Dáil. In 1999, she became the principal of the Harold School in Glasthule. In 2004, she was elected as a PD councillor on

Dún Laoghaire-Rathdown county council, swapping parties to join Fine Gael in December 2007. She has been a TD since 2011 and is currently Minister of State for Higher Education, a job to which she was appointed in June 2017. She is divorced and has two sons from her marriage.

DEREK MULLIGAN

Derek Mulligan, a retired estate agent from Blackrock, showed his keen interest in classic car racing by taking part in the 2003 Euroclassic run from Antwerp to Vienna. He was at the wheel of the oldest Irish entry, a 1954 XK 140 Jaguar, together with Bill Riordan.

COLIN O'DALY

A well-known chef, who has since become as noted for his paintings, Colin O'Daly once had a close connection with Blackrock.

Born in 1952, a native of Dublin's Northside, he started his career in the catering business at the age of 16 in the restaurant at Dublin airport when it was being run by Johnny Oppermann. He eventually moved to Ashford Castle in Co Mayo, then to the Renvyle House hotel in Co Galway and the Park Hotel in Kenmare. From 1985 onwards, Colin ran the very successful Park restaurant on Main Street in Blackrock, but it eventually went into liquidation in a recessionary squeeze by his bank.

O'Daly lost two of his four children to cystic fibrosis and has never been blessed with robust health himself, but he has always been a fighter. After the closure of Park, he picked himself up and went on to become chef patron at Roly's inimitable bistro when it opened in Ballsbridge in 1992. It is still going strong today, although O'Daly left in 2009, becoming an adviser to other restaurants and turning his attention to developing his career as a painter.

SIR WILLIAM ORPEN

Sir William Orpen (1878–1931), lived in a house called Oriel on Grove Avenue, just off Mount Merrion Avenue. He became a leading portrait painter in the early twentieth century and was also an official war artist during the First World War. Some of his work is on permanent display in the National Gallery of Ireland. Among his most famous works was his portrait of Lady Lavery, used on early Irish bank notes issued in the 1920s. Orpen has been commemorated with an enormous sculpture created by Blackrock sculptor Rowan Gillespie. This was originally destined for the Stillorgan shopping centre, but after its new American owners turned down the statue it found a resting place outside the Talbot Hotel on the main road at Stillorgan.

SEAN O'SULLIVAN

Sean O'Sullivan (1906–64) was a noted painter of his time, who lived for many years at Avoca Avenue, Blackrock.

He had studied art in Dublin, before moving first to London and then to Paris, to do the same in those cities. In Paris, he became very friendly with Samuel Beckett and James Joyce.

O'Sullivan moved back to Dublin in the late 1920s. He had begun exhibiting at the Royal Hibernian Academy in 1926, and for many years subsequently he exhibited an average of six paintings a year – portraits as well as landscapes painted in the west of Ireland.

O'Sullivan painted portraits of many famous artistic figures, including Brendan Behan, James Joyce and W.B. Yeats, as well as political and philanthropic figures such as Éamon de Valera and Sir Chester Beatty.

PROBY FAMILY

The Proby family has had a long connection with Blackrock, and Proby Square, on the upper part of Carysfort Avenue, is named after them.

The first member of the family to have a close association with the area was John Joshua Proby (1751–1828), who became the first Earl of Carysfort. He was a well-known politician and supporter of the arts in his day, although he didn't live in Blackrock. The main residence for the family was Glenart Castle in the Vale of Avoca in Co Wicklow. In time, a descendant, Granville Proby (1883–1947) continued the development of the family's Carysfort estates. His name lives on in Granville Park, beside the Proby walled orchard and fruit garden, and Granville Road, off Newtownpark Avenue.

The next Proby to come to prominence in the area was Claud Proby (1917–87), who was a captain in the Irish Guards during the Second World War. After the war, he came to live in a big house called Eversham, at the top of Newtownpark Avenue and from there, managed his estates in Newtown as well as in Dalkey.

In 1960, however, he suffered from adverse publicity over litigation concerning tenants' rights. After his death, his son James, who was born in 1944, decided not to live in Eversham, which was sold to a religious order and became a liturgical centre.

THE QUAKERS

The Quakers, full of entrepreneurial zest and a commitment to good works, were both numerous and influential in nineteenth-century Blackrock.

They were careful and frugal landowners who moved into trade, becoming wool merchants, millers and grain merchants. They went into other areas, too, like tea retailing and shipping, and their honesty in business proved a valuable calling card. The Quakers also brought these same principles to the insurance business and to merchant banking. The money that they earned was invested in many fine houses in the Blackrock area, usually surrounded by considerable gardens. So numerous was the Quaker community in the area that it came as no surprise when they opened a meeting house and a burial place at Temple Hill in 1860.

Since they had such strictly held religious beliefs, they preferred to live in close-knit communities and to marry within the Quaker fold, so a considerable Quaker community flourished in the Blackrock area, including in Newtownpark. By the middle of the nineteenth century, Quaker families living in the Newtownpark area included the Allens, the Bewleys, the Eustaces, the Goodbodys, the Hoggs, the Perrys, the Pims and the Williams.

One of the most powerful Quaker businessmen who lived in Blackrock was Samuel Bewley, who was born in 1764. His father was Thomas Bewley and his mother was Susanna Pim, a member of the Pim family who were so powerful in business and financial circles in Dublin in the nineteenth century.

As for Samuel, he started off as a silk merchant, importing fine silks from Italy, the Middle East and London. He became a major shareholder in the Mining Company of Ireland and was also very involved in the National Assurance company. He was also instrumental in starting up the Dublin Savings Bank.

He died in 1837 and was survived by five sons and one daughter. One of his children was Joshua Bewley, who started the renowned Bewley tea shops and cafés in 1840. Two other

Bewleys who had close connections with the Newtownpark area were John and Thomas Bewley, who owned and ran the Bewley & Webb shipyard on the North Wall, one of Dublin's leading shipbuilders in the mid-nineteenth century.

P.J. RUTTLEDGE

P.J. Ruttledge (1892–1952) came from Co Mayo, qualified as a solicitor and was then active in the 1919–1921 war of independence. In 1926, he was one of the founders of the Fianna Fáil party and when it came to power in 1932, he went on to hold various ministerial appointments. By 1940, he was Minister for Local Government and Public Health; he and his family lived at Ardagh Park, just off Newtownpark Avenue. His health deteriorated, however, forcing him to step down as a minister in 1941, eleven years before he died.

MARGOT SLATTERY

Margot Slattery, one of the best-known figures in the catering industry in Ireland, comes from Limerick but lives in Blackrock. In 2014 she was named by OUTstanding and the *Financial Times* as the most important business figure in the lesbian, gay, bisexual and transgender community in Ireland. In 2018, she was described by the Women's Executive Network as being one of the most powerful women in Ireland.

Slattery studied catering at the Galway Mayo Institute of Technology, then hospitality administration at the Dublin Institute of Technology. She worked for several hotels in both Ireland and the UK before being appointed the first female

CEO of Sodexa Ireland, a leading French-owned catering company, in 2012. It now employs close-on 2,000 people in Ireland; its head office is in the centre of Blackrock and, as one of the largest catering operators in Ireland, it supplies more than 90,000 meals each day across more than 200 different client locations.

JOHN STAFFORD

John Stafford was one of the founders of the Blackrock Society, which has flourished for nearly thirty years now in promoting interest in the history of the Blackrock area.

The idea for the Blackrock Society came from Stafford himself and it quickly came to fruition with the help of other enthusiasts in the Blackrock area. He was also the editor of the society's annual proceedings, which he saw grow from a slim sixty-page volume to a substantial 200-page book. Stafford was a skilled photographer and he supplied many of the photographs for the book himself. He also liked to commission the work of local artists such as Peter Pearson, Piet Sluis and Hugh Brady.

Stafford was also very energetic in his latter years in organising Bloomsday in Blackrock, with performances by such celebrities as Anthony Cronin, Ulick O'Connor and Maureen Charlton, in front of the old cross on Main Street.

Stafford wasn't a native of Blackrock; he was born in Birmingham in 1934 and his father came to Ireland as a senior representative for the Kodak company, which helped explain his son's great interest in photography. Stafford's maternal grandparents came from Romania and France, while his maternal grandfather was a couturier who had once worked at the Russian imperial court and was said to have been tailor for one of the tsars. Stafford himself was schooled at the Catholic Oratory in Birmingham and later graduated from UCD with a Bsc.

He worked first for the Gypsum company in Co Cavan and spent the rest of his career working in the laboratories of a number of Dublin hospitals, including Sir Patrick Dun's, Harcourt Street Children's Hospital, and finally, at the end of his career, at St James's Hospital, from which he retired in 1999. Apart from his great interest in the history of Blackrock, Stafford was also devoted to sailing, while he was a keen cook.

Stafford married Catherine O'Brien, from whom he later separated; they had three daughters, Jane, Emma and Lucy. He died in November 2005 aged 70, and was survived by his former wife, Catherine, and his three daughters.

JAMES STEPHENS

James Stephens was a well-known nineteenth-century agitator for Irish independence; for part of his adult life, he lived at 82 George's Avenue in Blackrock.

Stephens came from Kilkenny, where he was born in 1825. His father worked as a clerk for William Douglas Jackson's firm of auctioneers and booksellers in Kilkenny city. The young Stephens soon became indoctrinated with the quest for Irish freedom and took a leading role in the 1848 rebellion. After it collapsed, he escaped to France, where he spent seven years in exile. In 1856, he returned to Ireland and set about completing an incredible 4,800km walk around Ireland to meet as many people as possible. Two years later, in 1858, he was instrumental in founding the Irish Republican Brotherhood, originally known as the Irish Revolutionary Brotherhood, at Peter Lanigan's timber yard in Lombard Street near Dublin city centre. The organisation was also founded in America at around the same time.

Later, in 1863, when the *Irish People* newspaper was founded, Stephens became the editor. Two years later, many leaders of the Fenian movement were arrested, but two days earlier, Stephens had managed to escape from Richmond prison in Dublin and make his way to France, where he began his second period in exile. He eventually made his way back to Dublin, where he died in 1901.

DOT TUBRIDY

Dot Tubridy, who died in May 2018, had a long friendship with the Kennedy family in the US and was one of the main inspirations for the visit to Ireland in June 1963 of then-president John F. Kennedy. She was an aunt to RTÉ presenter Ryan Tubridy.

She was born Dorothy Lawlor, one of eleven children, in a Co Kilkenny family. Dot went on to marry Michael Tubridy, from Co Clare, a captain in the Irish army. He was a champion GAA footballer and went on to find fame as an international showjumping champion. After he retired from the army, he became manager of a stud in Co Meath owned by Seamus McGrath. The McGrath family not only owned and controlled the Irish Hospitals Sweepstakes but also other businesses, such as Waterford Crystal.

Sadly, Michael was killed in a horse riding accident at the age of 31, leaving Dot as a young widow with a three-month-old daughter, Áine. The McGraths then put her in charge of marketing at Waterford Crystal. In the US, working for the crystal firm, she developed a close friendship with the Kennedy family. She accompanied Kennedy on his 1963 Irish visit. Much later, in 1985, she was one of the founders in Ireland of the Special Olympics, which had been founded in the US by her friend Eunice Shriver.

Back home in Dublin, she was well-known on the city's social scene. She lived for many years in Rathgar, but later on lived at the Elms apartment complex in Blackrock.

RYAN TUBRIDY

Ryan Tubridy, one of the best-known TV and radio presenters with RTÉ, was born in Booterstown on 28 May 1973 but grew up in Blackrock. He was educated at Carysfort national school in Blackrock, then at Blackrock College and finally at UCD.

His father, Patrick, was a medical practitioner in Blackrock. He himself was the only son of a Fianna Fáil Deputy, Seán Tubridy, also a medical practitioner, who died in 1939 aged 42. His mother is Catherine Andrews, whose father, Todd Andrews, was in charge of Bord na Móna for many years and then became chairman of the RTÉ Authority. Catherine and Patrick had five children together, and Patrick had two more with his second wife, Adela. Patrick died in January 2013.

As for Ryan, he began broadcasting at the tender age of 12, reviewing books for the *Poparama* show on 2FM, presented by Ruth Buchanan, now retired, the wife of transport minister Shane Ross. Ryan began his own show on Radio 1 in 2006, until 2010, when he moved to 2FM. He returned to Radio 1 in 2015 with the weekday morning show named after him. Since 2009, he has also been the presenter on TV's *The Late Late Show*.

ÉAMON DE VALERA

Both a long-serving Taoiseach and president of Ireland, Éamon de Valera was the foremost political figure in twentieth-century Ireland, and had close connections with Blackrock.

Between 1898 and 1900, the young de Valera completed his secondary education at Blackrock College and then lived on campus there for a further three years, until 1903, while he studied at the old Royal University of Ireland, predecessor of the present-day National University of Ireland. He lived on Williamstown Avenue before eventually moving to Merrion View Avenue in Merrion in 1908.

De Valera returned to Blackrock College as a maths teacher, and he also taught at the old Our Lady of Mercy teacher training college in Blackrock. He married Sinéad Flanagan, a teacher from Balbriggan, in 1910 and they lived briefly at Vernon Terrace in Booterstown. Later on, after he had become president in 1932, the family moved in 1933 to Herberton, a grand house on Cross Avenue. It was in this house that much of the 1937 constitution was drafted.

MAURICE WALSH

Maurice Walsh (1879–1964), hailed from Listowel, Co Kerry. At an early age, he started work with Customs & Excise in Scotland; eventually, in 1922, at the start of the Irish Free State, he transferred to the new Irish Customs & Excise service. He spent just over a decade in that job, retiring in 1933.

Long before he retired, however, he had started enjoying success as a novelist and short story writer. His most famous short story was *The Quiet Man*, which was turned into the

1952 film of the same name, starring John Wayne and Maureen O'Hara. In his later years, Walsh lived in the Blackrock area, at Stillorgan Park Avenue and at Avoca Road. He died in Blackrock on 18 February 1964.

T.P. WHELEHAN

T.P. Whelehan was a colourful character who lived in Avoca Road, Blackrock, for many years, a noted wine correspondent.

He came from Mullingar, where his father Kevin ran a pharmacy. Whelehan went to Blackrock College, then to UCD, where he studied pharmacy. He then returned to Mullingar where he joined his father in the fast-expanding family business, which became a leading distributor of pharmaceutical products. The firm was sold in the 1990s.

Whelehan also had an encyclopaedic knowledge of wine, which he put to good use as wine correspondent for *The Irish Times* from 1960 until 1987, where his enthusiasm for his subject often bubbled over into eloquent and often poetic prose. He was also the wine consultant for the old Quinnworth, now Tesco, for a decade.

Apart from wine, Whelehan also had a huge enthusiasm for gardening, reflected in the marvellous garden he and his wife Anne tended at their home in Blackrock. He even became an international judge of roses.

Whelehan died in 2016 and was survived by Anne and their three children, Rebecca, Kevin and David, as well as by his two brothers, Richard and Harry, and his sisters Helen and Hilda. He often referred to himself and his brothers as 'Tom, Dick and Harry'. His two sons both work in the wine business, Kevin in Japan and David in his retail shop at

Loughlinstown, south Co Dublin, located in what was once the Silver Tassie pub.

THE OLD BOYS' CLUB

Since it was founded as the French College in 1860, Blackrock College has produced an enormous number of alumni – otherwise known as the Old Rockmen – who have gone on to achieve great heights in their chosen profession. Probably more so than any other private, fee-paying secondary school in Ireland, Blackrock College has produced the greatest number of pupils who have risen to the highest echelons in Irish society, the 'crème de la crème'. A selection of their lives are featured here.

Academic

Bryan Patrick Beirne (1918–98) emigrated to Canada in 1949, where he became a world expert on pest control.

Alfred O' Rahilly (1884–1966) was a TD for Cork city before being made president of University College, Cork, a position he held from 1943 until 1954.

Arts

Robert Ballagh, born in Dublin in 1943, has become perhaps the most outstanding artist of his generation in Ireland, with a highly distinctive style. He has been a painter, a print maker, a designer and a set designer by turn, as well as a political activist.

Paul Costelloe, born in Dublin in 1945, is a noted fashion designer in both Ireland and Britain.

Fergus Martin is a well-known painter and sculptor.

Michael McGlynn, born in Dublin in 1964, is a noted composer, producer, director and founder of the vocal ensemble Anúna.

Rónán Murray, born in Dublin in 1973, is a well-known organist, pianist and composer.

Pauric Sweeney, born in Co Donegal in 1973, started off as a jewellery designer, but is now best-known for his handbags.

Business

Eddie O'Connor is founder and CEO of Airtricity, a big name in renewable energy resources.

Dr Brendan O'Regan was the businessman who transformed Shannon Airport, especially through its duty free sales and free trade zone. More recently, he was closely involved in the peace process in Ireland.

David J. O'Reilly is chairman and CEO of the Chevron Foundation.

Derek Quinlan is a former tax specialist turned property investor.

Lochlann Quinn is a co-founder of the Glen Dimplex group and a former chair of AIB.

Clergy

John, Cardinal D'Alton (1882–1963), was a former Archbishop of Armagh and Primate of All Ireland.

Robert Ellison, born in 1942, was bishop of Banjui in Gambia from 2006 to 2017.

Michael Joseph Moloney (1912–91) also had a spell as Bishop of Banjul in Gambia, preceding Robert Ellison.

John Charles McQuaid was Catholic Archbishop of Dublin from 1940 to 1972 and the most powerful Catholic prelate in Ireland at the time. He was highly controversial and had many peculiar obsessions, such as the moral hazards of women using Tampax. He had also been president of Blackrock College between 1931 and 1939. He did good work supporting starving artists however, such as poet Patrick Kavanagh.

Donal Murray, born in 1940, was Bishop of Limerick from 1996 to 2009.

Joseph Brendan Whelan (1909–90) was Bishop of Owerri in Nigeria from 1950 to 1970, when he was deported from Nigeria during the civil war there.

Entertainment

Des Bishop, is a well-known TV comedian.

Craig Doyle is a TV presenter in both Ireland and Britain.

Dave Fanning is a long-time music presenter with RTÉ's 2FM.

Conal Gallen is a comedian, playwright and singer/songwriter.

Bob Geldof was the lead singer of the Boomtown Rats and organiser of Live Aid concerts, and has been involved in other humanitarian work.

Frank Kelly (1938–2016) was an actor, best known as Father Jack, the totally obnoxious old priest in the *Father Ted* TV comedy series.

David McSavage is a TV comedian and writer. His real name is David Andrews Junior, and he is a member of the Andrews political dynasty.

Ardal O'Hanlon is a TV comic actor.

Ryan Tubridy is a radio presenter on RTÉ's Radio 1 and a presenter of *The Late Late Show* on RTÉ One television.

Humanitarian

Frank Duff (1889–1980), was the founder of the Legion of Mary in Dublin in 1921. Today, it has 4 million active members and 10 million auxiliary members, in nearly 200 countries. It is represented in almost every Catholic diocese in the world.

Niall O'Brien was an Irish Columban missionary priest well known for his work in the Philippines; he died in 2004.

Journalism

Rory Carroll is a foreign reporter for *The Guardian* newspaper published in London. He gained international attention when he was kidnapped in Iraq in 2005 but he was later released unharmed.

Paddy Murray was editor of the old *Sunday Tribune* newspaper from 2002 to 2005.

David McWilliams is a prolific journalist and broadcaster on the subject of economics and, according to his own website, the tenth most influential economist in the world.

Paul Tansey was the economics editor of *The Irish Times*; he died in 2008 and is survived by his wife, Emily O'Reilly, who is a well-known writer and broadcaster.

Literature

Phádraic Ó Conaire (1882–1928) was a writer and journalist who wrote in Irish, especially about the plight of Irish emigrants. He is commemorated by a statue in Eyre Square in his native Galway. He spent the last years of his life there, eking out a meagre existence from his writings, and died destitute in a Dublin hospital in 1928.

Tim Pat Coogan, who is now 84, was a journalist for many years and last but one editor of the old *Irish Press*, between 1968 and 1987. After leaving journalism, he turned his hand to writing historical narratives.

Conal Gallen was born in Derry but grew up in Co Donegal. Now 63, he co-wrote various farces with his son Rory and, for the past thirty years, has been one of Ireland's top performers.

Paul Murray, born in 1975, is an accomplished contemporary novelist, the author of such works as *Skippy Dies* (2010) and *The Mark and the Void* (2015).

Joseph O'Connor had been a journalist but turned to writing fiction, a wise decision confirmed by his outstanding 2002 novel, *Star of the Sea*.

Liam O'Flaherty (1896–1984) was a noted novelist and short story writer, best known for his work *The Informer*.

Brian O'Nolan (1911–66) was a novelist who wrote such outstanding works of satire as *At Swim-Two-Birds* (1939) and *The Third Policeman* (1967), under the *nom de plume* of Flann O'Brien. Under another *nom de plume*, Myles na gCopaleen, he wrote a satirical column, *Cruiskeen Lawn*, for *The Irish Times* from 1940 until his death in 1966. He also had a day job in the civil service as the Secretary of the Department of Local Government. He was an alcoholic for most of his adult life and was also notorious for never standing his round.

Legal

Seamus Egan was a former judge in the Supreme Court; he died in 2004.

Dermot Gleeson, a former Attorney General, was appointed chair of AIB in 2003.

Ronan Keane, born in 1932, was the Chief Justice of the Supreme Court in Ireland between 2000 and 2004. He was married to the late Terry Keane, social diarist, who was also the mistress of a former Taoiseach, Charles Haughey. Justine, the daughter of Ronan and Terry Keane, is married to Diarmuid Gavin, the garden designer and TV personality.

Michael Moriarty was appointed a High Court judge in 1994, then when the Moriarty Tribunal started in 1997 to enquire into payments to politicians, he was its chair. The tribunal was very long running; its final report wasn't published until 2011.

John Quirke was a High Court judge between 1997 and 2012.

Politics

Barry Andrews was a TD for Dún Laoghaire from 2002 until 2011, and from 2008 until 2011, served as minister for children.

Michael Collins joined what is now the Department of Foreign Affairs and Trade in 1974. He was appointed Irish ambassador to the US in 2007, and in 2013 became ambassador to Germany.

James MacMahon (1865–1954) was appointed Secretary for Ireland in 1918 but retired when the Irish Free State came into being. In 1928, he was made president of the RDS.

James McNeill was the first Irish high commissioner in London after the Irish Free State was set up, then became second governor-general of the Irish Free State from 1927 until 1932.

Niall Ó Brolcháin was mayor of Galway from 2006 to 2007.

Rory O'Hanlon was a TD for Cavan-Monaghan from 1977 until 2011. He also held a number of Cabinet positions and was also Ceann Comhairle of Dáil Éireann.

Ruairi Quinn was minister for finance between 1994 and 1997 and went on to become leader of the Labour Party from 1997 until 2002.

Éamon de Valera was one of the key figures in the War of Independence between 1919 and 1921. Later, he headed up the government of Ireland six times. After his 1937 Constitution became law, his job title changed to Taoiseach. After he retired from that post in 1959, he went on to serve two terms as president of Ireland. He died in 1975. As a second level student, he had studied for two years at Blackrock College and later returned there to teach maths.

Vivion de Valera (1910–82) was the eldest son of Éamon de Valera and his wife, Sineád. Vivion was a TD from 1945 until 1981 and he was also the managing director of the old *Irish Press* newspaper group from 1951 until 1982.

Sport

Niall Brophy was one of the great Irish rugby stars of the 1950s and 60s.

Michael Cusack, founder of the Gaelic Athletic Association in 1884, was a teacher at Blackrock College.

Paul Dunne is a well-known golfer.

Michael Darragh MacAuley is a noted Dublin GAA footballer.

Brendan Mullin was an outstanding rugby player of the 1980s and 1990s, one of the best produced by Ireland.

Ryle Nugent ,a former head of sport at RTÉ, is a rugby commentator for RTÉ television.

Brian O'Driscoll was at Blackrock College from 1992 to 1998 and learned to play rugby there. From 2003 until 2012, he was captain of the Irish national rugby union team. Now, in retirement from the game, he is regarded as one of the greatest rugby players of all time, not just in Ireland, but worldwide. He married the TV actor Amy Huberman in 2010.

Cian O'Sullivan is a highly regarded Dublin Gaelic footballer.

John Quirke was an Irish international rugby player from 1962 to 1968 and he also became a High Court judge.

Nicholas Roche was born in 1984, the son of champion cyclist Stephen Roche, a winner of the Tour de France. Nicholas himself has gone on to win many awards in his professional cycling career.

Alain Rolland is an Irish international rugby and an international rugby referee.

Fergus Slattery was a famed Irish rugby player in the 1970s, one of the participants in the legendary Lions 1974 tour.

Mark Vaughan is a noted Dublin GAA footballer.

11

SCHOOLS AND COLLEGES

ALL SAINTS NATIONAL SCHOOL

Situated at the corner of Carysfort Avenue and Stillorgan Park, this Church of Ireland school was founded in 1879. A much-needed extension was built and opened in 1993. The school has about fifty-five pupils aged between 4 and 12, and the small number of pupils makes the school, which has three teachers, as child-centred as possible.

BENINCASA SPECIAL SCHOOL

Benincasa Special School in Blackrock enrols children aged between 5 and 16 who have special needs that can't be met by mainstream education. The children experience extra-curricular dance, drama, music, sports and other subjects, and new areas of talent are identified, which are nurtured and developed as the child either moves back to mainstream education or progresses to second level. The enrolment at the school in 2017/18 was forty-three boys and one girl.

BLACKROCK COLLEGE

Blackrock College is one of the best-known fee-paying Catholic secondary schools in Ireland. Its students are boys aged between 13 and 18, and the fees are considerable, around €7,000 a year for day students and about €18,000 a year for boarders.

The college dates back to 1860, when a French religious order, the Congregation of the Holy Ghost, set up the first of five schools in Ireland. The founder was Father Jules Leman, a French missionary priest, and for many years, the college in Blackrock was known as the French College. It had two aims, to train people for missionary work and to provide a first-class Catholic education for boys.

It was never a seminary but for over forty years, the college provided training for entrants to the civil service and the universities. In time, however, as University College Dublin grew, it superseded university studies in Blackrock.

For many years, the college had a strong clerical influence. John Charles McQuaid, who eventually became the Catholic Archbishop of Dublin and a very controversial figure, had joined the staff of Blackrock College as a teacher in 1925 and eventually, from 1931 until 1939, he was its president.

Today, the college has around 1,000 students, with close on ninety teachers working in twenty-one departments. The most popular specialisations, in order, are Biology, French, Geography, Business, History and Accounting. All but about 5 per cent of its students go on to third-level studies. In addition to all the day pupils, the college has about 100 boarders, who live in the 1780 Williamstown Castle on campus.

Blackrock College is also well-known for its sporting prowess, especially in rugby union, and many past and present pupils have learned their rugby skills at the college, including the former Ireland captain, Brian O'Driscoll.

The college has also had many notable teachers, and many past pupils have also distinguished themselves – see the *Old Boys' Club* section in Chapter 10 of this book.

St Andrew's College is equally renowned in the area as a second-level college, as well as for its junior school, but it is based in Booterstown.

BLACKROCK EDUCATION CENTRE

The Blackrock Education Centre was established in 1972 to provide support for teachers and others involved in education in about 250 schools, with about 5,000 teachers in what is now the Dún Laoghaire-Rathdown county council area.

This centre was set up at Carysfort Avenue in Blackrock and stayed there for nearly twenty-five years. In 1996, it moved to the grounds of the Institute of Art, Design and Technology, Dún Laoghaire, at Deansgrange.

BLACKROCK FURTHER EDUCATION INSTITUTE

The new Blackrock Further Education Institute opened in September 2015, after an investment of €9.5 million in the new campus. The principal of the new institute is Tom Taylor, who succeeded original principal Deirdre Hanamy, and it opened with over 1,000 full- and part-time students, making it one of the largest further education colleges in Ireland.

The institute was formerly Senior College, Dún Laoghaire. The new institute is located on the site of the original town hall, the Carnegie Library and the Municipal Technical College in Blackrock. The original nineteenth- and early twentieth-century structures were incorporated into the new development, which also includes the recently refurbished and much extended Blackrock library, which is run by the library service of Dún Laoghaire-Rathdown county council. The original library was built in 1905, with the help of a £3,000 grant from Andrew Carnegie, the Scottish–American philanthropist. The new development has two courtyards, one open, the other glazed. Designed by McCullough Mulvin architects and built by Collen Construction, the new building doesn't have a formal entrance – this is preserved in the old town hall.

The features of the original late nineteenth-century and early twentieth-century protected structures were incorporated into the new development, including part of the front of the old Blackrock fire station. The new campus took joint first place in the 2014 Irish Georgian Society Conservation Awards and was named Educational Project of the Year in the 2014 Irish Construction Awards.

The new institute has state-of-the-art computer labs, design studios, beauty salons, an information and technology centre and a café. More than fifty day and evening courses are offered at levels five and six, for both school leavers and adults returning to education. The courses cover a wide range of subjects, from accounting and beauty therapy to computing and creative technologies as well as emergency services and healthcare.

One of its most popular courses has been a ten-week module in Criminology, aimed at people with an interest in criminal law and crime scene investigation. Elements of the €180 course include examining the nature of criminal behaviour and gathering crime scene evidence.

Deirdre Hanamy said at the time of the institute's opening that the new premises would enhance their ability to provide a quality teaching and learning experience. She added that the new institute in Blackrock, along with similar educational establishments, have a significant role to play in the education and upskilling of future generations of workers, as well as a responsibility to ensure that courses remain industry-relevant, quality assured, accessible and affordable.

BLACKROCK SCOUTS

The twenty-ninth Dublin Scouts were founded in 1940 by Peter Pender and have been going strong ever since. The scout den, which is close to the sea and to Seapoint railway station, was recently redeveloped.

BOOTERSTOWN NATIONAL SCHOOL

This Church of Ireland school is in the grounds of St Philip and St James's church on Cross Avenue, near its junction with Mount Merrion Avenue. Its principal is Rachel Fraser and it has an active parent-teacher association. The school garden is used to grow fruit and vegetables and has strong green credentials; it is now on its third green flag.

CARYSFORT COLLEGE

This was an important primary teacher training centre based in Blackrock from its inception in 1877 until its closure in 1988.

It was founded by the Sisters of Mercy and over the years it became a leading centre in Ireland for training teachers.

In 1975, major reforms in the education system saw the college become part of the National University of Ireland, along with other teacher training centres. The college then started awarding the BEd degree, as well as offering a postgraduate qualification in primary school teaching. In 1982, a new library, a 700-seat auditorium, a sports centre and an audio-visual centre were opened, but six years later, the college closed. For the last graduation ceremony in October 1988, Seamus Heaney, a former teacher and head of the English department there, composed valedictory verses. Another luminary who taught at the old college was Éamon de Valera.

In 1991, much of the estate, together with the main buildings, were sold to UCD for £8 million, and the old college became the Michael Smurfit Graduate Business School.

CARYSFORT NATIONAL SCHOOL

This national school was established by the Sisters of Mercy in 1895 and is on Convent Road, just off Carysfort Avenue. It borders the grounds of the UCD Smurfit Business School. The principal is Norma Linehan and the co-educational school is under the patronage of the Catholic Archbishop of Dublin.

BRONWYN CONROY

This establishment, which provides a wide range of beauty courses, dates back to 1972 and has its Dublin base at Temple Hall on the Temple Road.

DOMINICAN COLLEGE, SION HILL

Dominican College, Sion Hill, is one of the oldest girls' secondary schools in Ireland, dating back to 1836, when it was founded by the Dominican Sisters in a suburban villa called Sion Hill. It acquired this name because the previous owners of the house had brought back many rare shrubs from the Holy Land.

Initially, the school had forty day pupils, eight boarders and ten nuns. By 1950, it had 120 day pupils and 130 boarders. The boarding school closed in the late 1960s and Dominican College now has 500 day pupils. Under principal Sheila Drum, there are close on thirty teachers, as well as special needs assistants.

The school used to have two grass hockey pitches, but these were sold off in 1990 for housing development. In 2008, the concert hall, which had been built in 1928, was modernised. It is well-known for its musical activities, and the music department offers Music at Junior and Leaving Certificate level, while the school also has three voluntary choirs and an orchestra.

Dominican College also offers a wide range of sports, including archery, athletics, basketball, Highland Games and tennis. It is particularly noted for its prowess in hockey, with professionally coached teams taking part in the Leinster Schoolgirls' competitions.

DUBLIN COOKERY SCHOOL

This cookery school, run by Lynda Booth, is based at Brookfield Terrace in Blackrock, where it has state-of-the-art facilities, extending to nearly 300m^2. A wide range of evening and one-day courses are offered, as well as full-time courses lasting one week and one month. In addition, there is a three-month professional course. The premises are also promoted as an ideal venue for parties and cookery events.

EARLY NINETEENTH-CENTURY SCHOOLS

In the early nineteenth century, long before the national school system was established, Blackrock had several fee-paying establishments whose pupils came from the well-to-do citizens of Blackrock, but not from the poorer classes. These schools included a classical and mercantile academy, an English-style grammar school, and Dr Miller's Academy. In the Newtownpark area during that same period, two schools were established.

An evangelical banker called Charles Doyne (1775–1857) established and paid for a schoolhouse on Newtownpark Avenue; later, it was turned into a house called Belclare. Then, just off the top of Newtownpark Avenue, a Dr Smyth established a boarding school called Belmont Boarding School, which survived for much of the nineteenth century.

GUARDIAN ANGELS NATIONAL SCHOOL

This co-educational primary school was opened in 1970, two years after the adjacent parish church was consecrated. Pádraig O'Neill is the principal, and it is under the patronage of the Catholic Archbishop of Dublin, although it welcomes pupils of all denominations. It has very child-centred curriculum and a wide range of extracurricula activities.

When the school first opened, it was in a series of wooden pre-fab buildings, which includes six classrooms. In 1978, however, the first of the new buildings was opened and in the 1990s, a completely new school was built on the site. Today, the school has twelve classrooms.

INTERNATIONAL SCHOOL OF IRELAND

This was established in 2007 at Barclay Court on the Temple Road in Blackrock to meet the need for educational diversity in Ireland. Its students are aged from 3 to 12 and represent over twenty different nationalities. It is the only accredited IB World Primary School in Ireland and it is a small, private, non-profit school that is co-educational, non-denominational and culturally diverse.

MEATH INDUSTRIAL SCHOOL

In recent years, industrial schools have been widely discredited because of the way children in their care were treated.

Blackrock once had a leading industrial school, however, for Protestant boys. It was founded in 1871 by the Earl of Meath, hence its name. It was in a large house on Rock Hill called Elm Hill, subsequently subsumed into Blackrock Park. The school opened on 5 May 1871, with twelve boys in residence. They received a good Scriptural education, as well as being taught shoe making and tailoring. The boys made shoes for themselves, as well as for other similar institutions, and for the general public.

The lease on Elm Cliff expired in 1876 and the original plan then was to build a new school at Merrion, close to Sydney Parade railway station, but this never materialised. Instead, a four-hectare site was established at Carysfort Avenue, Blackrock, and a school was built there. Buying the land and building the school cost £6,000, which put the school in debt for many years.

The new school opened in April 1877. It had a capacity of 100 places and the new premises included a dairy, a cow house and stables. The boys, in addition to their education, worked in the farm garden and carried out all the household duties of the school. By 1902, the number of places had been increased to 150 and in 1911 it was reported that the school had sixteen boys trained as tailors, fifteen as shoemakers, eight as carpenters, two as painters, and twenty-five as agriculturalists.

In March 1917, during the First World War, the premises were taken over for use as a military orthopaedic hospital and the boys were transferred to Balmoral Industrial School in Belfast. The Blackrock school never reopened and today the premises survive as part of a business park.

MICHAEL SMURFIT GRADUATE BUSINESS SCHOOL

This is the graduate business school of UCD and it was set up on the site of the old Carysfort teacher training college in Blackrock. It is named after its main benefactor, the businessman Michael Smurfit. Another leading businessman, Denis O'Brien, is also a major benefactor. Its MBA programmes are highly rated; in 2015, the *Financial Times* ranked the school seventy-third in the world's MBA programme providers, and forty-first in Europe.

The school offers programmes for Masters in such subjects as Accountancy, Finance, Human Resource Management, many other areas of management, marketing and technology and innovation. A few of its courses are run not in Blackrock, but on the UCD campus in Belfield.

Many people who have graduated from the school have subsequently come to prominence in business life, both in Ireland and elsewhere. A few of its well-known alumni include Sarah Carey, broadcaster and columnist; Conor McNamara, sports commentator; Derval O' Rourke, athlete; Nóirin O' Sullivan, a former Garda Commissioner; and Julie-Ann Russell, footballer.

NEWPARK COMPREHENSIVE SCHOOL

This non-fee-paying, coeducational comprehensive school, under Church of Ireland management, opened on Newtownpark Avenue in 1972. It provides post-primary education for the Church of Ireland community in south Co Dublin and north Co Wicklow, and it combined two earlier schools, the Avoca School set up in 1891 at Avoca Place in Blackrock, and the Kingstown School, established in 1894 in what was then Kingstown, now Dún Laoghaire.

The campus covers 10 hectares and the school centres on a prefab-style block that opened in 1974, while two large houses on the site, Melfield and Belfort, were also used. In 2015, a new

school building was opened and many of the ancilliary rooms were demolished, leaving only these two big houses from the original plan. The sports centre, built in 1973, has been developed into a multi-purpose facility that is also available for the local community. Students at Newpark have shown particular prowess in hockey.

Other facilities include the music centre, which opened in 1978. It is now recognised as the main centre in Ireland for jazz-related musical education.

Notable teachers and alumni at the school include Bryan Dobson, RTÉ radio news presenter; the late Dr John de Courcy Ireland, maritime historian; David McCullagh, RTÉ journalist and author; and Mario Rosenstock, actor and comedian.

OUR LADY OF MERCY CONVENT SCHOOL

Located at Rosemount Terrace in Booterstown, Our Lady of Mercy's enrolment is 220 girls. The teacher-pupil ratio is one teacher for every eighteen pupils, and the principal of this Catholic-ethos school is Mairin Benson.

COLLEGE OF PROGRESSIVE EDUCATION

This college was founded in 1986 by Anne Clinch, a paediatric nurse, who indentified the need for quality training for childcare practitioners in Ireland. Its programmes are offered at its main centre in the UCD Smurfit Business School in Carysfort Avenue, as well as at other locations in Dublin and at regional locations throughout Ireland. Its head office is based at Rock Hill, Main Street, Blackrock.

ROSEMONT SECONDARY SCHOOL

This secondary school for girls, formerly at Temple Road, Blackrock, has an enrolment of around 300; it was inspired by the life and teachings of St Josemaria Escriva, the founder of Opus Dei. The school moved from Blackrock to Sandyford in 2012 and four years later, in 2016, the site in Blackrock was sold off for housing development.

ST AUGUSTINE'S SCHOOL

This school caters for children aged between 8 and 18 who have special educational needs, otherwise described as mild general learning disabilities. It has about 160 students in the primary, post-primary and vocational departments. The school is well equipped; facilities include an extensive modern computer suite, a large gym, a ceramics workshop, a library, domestic science rooms, a swimming pool, and outdoor facilities for basketball, football and tennis.

WILLOW PARK JUNIOR SCHOOL

With some 620 boys, Willow Park Junior School shares the Wiliamstown campus with Blackrock College and Willow Park First Year. The junior school is a Spiritan establishment that works with parents in the moral, social and intellectual formation of their children. As an independent junior school, Willow Park is fees dependent. Blackrock College, too, is a Spiritan establishment.

12
COMMUNITY ORGANISATIONS

BLACKROCK BUSINESS NETWORK

This very active business network deals with many issues that affect community and business life in Blackrock. It is made up of eight elected members and a number of co-opted members, all of whom give their time voluntarily. It is based at 6 Main Street, and its website, blackrock.ie, has a full list of companies that belong to the network.

BLACKROCK AND MONKSTOWN ACTIVE RETIREMENT ASSOCIATION

This very active association for older people living in the area meets every Thursday afternoon in the parish centre of St John the Baptist church in Blackrock. Activities include a book club, bridge, Italian classes and physical education. Outings, holidays and other events and activities are also organised.

BLACKROCK SOCIETY

The society organises talks and outings of a historical and literary nature and it holds its monthly meetings at Comhaltas Ceoltóiri Éireann, in Monkstown.

BLACKROCK TIDY TOWNS

A group of residents, traders and other interested parties set up the Tidy Towns committee in Blackrock in 2007 and the area entered the competition for the first time the following year. In 2012, it won two awards in the county Tidy Districts part of the competition, as well as taking second place in the Large Towns section. Blackrock has also done well in the Most Improved Towns category. All the awards won by Blackrock are on display in the Blackrock Centre.

FRASCATI SINGERS

This mixed-voice vocal group was set up in 2001 and with over thirty-five members, it meets regularly for choral practice during school terms at St Andrew's Presbyterian church hall on Mount Merrion Avenue. The singers perform a wide range of styles, including sacred, folk, popular, seasonal and modern, in a variety of languages. Under director Eunan McDonald, the Frascati Singers take part in many festivals and community events. Its annual Christmas concert in early December is always a popular event, staged in St Andrew's church. Another of its recent performances was of Verdi's *Gloria*, in All Saints church on Carysfort Avenue in May

2017. The singers are always looking for new members, especially basses and tenors.

ICA GUILD

Guilds in the Dublin area are organised into the Dublin Federation of the Irish Countrywomen's Association, and the Blackrock guild is particularly active.

It organises a varied programme of events and activities, including arts and crafts, interesting talks, trips and visits, competitions, and many other events in an action-packed calendar. The Blackrock Guild meets every month, on the second and fourth Thursday of the month between September and June, at the Holy Family Resource Centre in Kill o' the Grange.

URBAN JUNCTION

This is primarily an organisation that arranges social, educational and other activities for children, young people and adults in the wider Blackrock community. The Blackrock Community Play Group organises Montessori and nursery classes at Urban Junction s premises on Main Street, Blackrock.

13

SHOPS OLD AND NEW

ADAMS

The Adams salesrooms, nextdoor to the Bank of Ireland on Main Street, were founded in 1947 by Thomas P. Adams. Ever since then, Adams has been noted for its antique furniture, paintings, silver, jewellery and decorative items, a favourite place for antique lovers and antique dealers. In addition to its well-attended sales, Adams also offers in-situ home contents sales.

BLACKROCK AUTO CLINIC

Located at No.1, Sweetman's Avenue, Blackrock Auto Clinic has up-to-date diagnostic equipment for all makes and models of cars.

BLACKROCK BUILDERS PROVIDERS

Based on Brookfield Avenue, Blackrock Builders Providers offers a wide range of building materials and products for professional builders, plumbers and DIY enthusiasts, through its shop, trade counter and yard.

BLACKROCK CELLAR

After Oddbins closed its off-licence on Rock Hill in 2012, a Frenchman who had worked in the shop, Joel Durand, took it over and renamed it the Blackrock Cellar. It is a friendly, walk-in shop that also sells online. It has a considerable selection of wines – some 450 – as well as the same number of craft beer brands and plenty of spirits. It also offers a great selection of Spanish tapas.

BLACKROCK HAIRDRESSERS

In addition to Aidan Fitzgerald's award-winning salon on Main Street (see page 143), the Blackrock area has close on a dozen barbers and hairdressing salons.

These include Peter Mark in the Frascati shopping centre; Toni and Guy on Main Street (barbers and hairdressers); Mary's hairdressing salon on Brookfield Avenue; Noel Higgins hair salon on Carysfort Avenue; the Barber Shop on Main Street; and The Barber's Lounge in Blackrock Market.

BLACKROCK KITCHEN STUDIO

This has been trading since 1986, designing and fitting kitchens; its main base is at George's Avenue, just off Main Street in Blackrock, while it has another outlet at Ballymore Eustace, Co Kildare.

BLACKROCK MARKET

One of the best-regarded markets in the greater Dublin area, Blackrock Market, just off Main Street, has a lively atmosphere and unique character. It opened in 1996 and is open every weekend as well as on Bank Holiday Mondays. It has over thirty stalls, selling a wide variety of items – everything from books to furniture, vintage fashion and jewellery, even furniture for dolls' houses. It also sells a range of food and beverages and has a number of restaurants, from what was the very upmarket Heron & Grey to the more affordable 3 Leaves, and even a fish and chip shop. Generally, when the market is open, over fifty traders are in action there, so bargain hunters and people in search of the odd and the unusual can have a whale of a time.

BLACKROCK POST OFFICE

For many years, the old Edwardian post office on Main Street in Blackrock was a local landmark, built in the early years of the twentieth century. In 2003 it was closed, however, and the retail post office moved to a unit in the Frascati shopping centre, where it is still based – although in early 2019,doubts were being expressed as to whether this sub- post office was going to survive.. The old post office building is currently closed, awaiting planning approval for redevelopment.

BLACKROCK RARE BOOKS

This enticing bookshop on Main Street in Blackrock has been established since 2013. It was originally known as Broadford Books, but Tim Collie and his partner Tanya Walsh took over the running of it, firstly in Blackrock Market and more recently in its own shop. Tim and Tanya are both from Dublin, but had worked in England for a number of years before deciding to return to Ireland.

Tim's main interests are in antiquarian books, illustrated books, emphemera and original manuscripts, while Tanya is interested in drama, literature and youth fiction. Their wide range of stock reflects their many interests in the world of books.

BLACKROCK SHOPPING CENTRE

The Blackrock shopping centre (now The Blackrock Centre) was built in 1984, with a large Superquinn supermarket as the key retail element. Feargal Quinn, who once ran the Superquinn supermarket company, recalls that when they bought the site his brother-in-law ran the pub there in order to retain the licence. He also recalls that after they had bought the land, he would sit in his garden using Lego to work out the levels for the centre.

Superquinn has long since given way to Super Valu, which now runs the supermarket in the centre. In July 2017, Super Valu said that it could face huge losses there because of redevelopment works in and close to the centre, and a reduction in car parking spaces. A €10 million upgrade started in the second quarter of 2018 and it is scheduled to be ready by the middle of 2019. It will include a new roof, a new facade, more retail space and a new entrance off Frascati Road.

Friends First, which now owns the site, is also redeveloping the adjoining Enterprise House site; the original office building, dating back to the 1980s, was demolished in 2018. A brand new building, with five floors and 8,000m^2 of accommodation, is currently under construction and is due for completion in 2019. The entire building has already been let to Zurich Life Assurance on a twenty-year lease.

There is also another office block at the shopping centre – Trident House, a four-storey building over a basement – a total

of 1,700m^2 of office accommodation. It had been occupied for over thirty years by the Office of Public Works, but was substantially revamped during 2018.

As for the shopping centre itself, it has long had about forty retail outlets and commercial businesses, in addition to the main supermarket. Within the past two years, new tenants have included Lisa Perkins, women's fashions; Vanilla Pod restaurant; Esquires gourmet coffee house; and Mobile Fix, which sells phones, tablets and accessories.

CARRAIG BOOKS

Blackrock is noted for its new and antiquarian booksellers, none more so than Carraig Books, but sadly, this bookshop closed down in 2018 with the retirement of its owner, Sean Keegan.

Keegan's father, Alfred, had a number of bookshops in Dublin city centre and started the Blackrock concern in 1968 in a half-timbered house directly opposite the library;

the premises had formerly been Miranda's tearooms. Over the years, Keegan built up a vast collection of antiquarian books – some 100,000 in all – in both the shop and in several storerooms. The books covered an enormous variety of Irish subjects, fiction and non fiction. Keegan has said that Blackrock has always been a good area for buying books, although the bulk of the firm's business was always in mail order. After his retirement, Keegan's daughter Kathleen continues to run the bookselling operations, but on a limited scale.

Alfred Day also set up Blackrock Printers at the back of the bookshop and this continues, run by Lena, David and Philip Keegan. It produces a wide range of high-quality business, personal and promotional print items.

CARROLL & KINSELLA

This well-known car firm, which has held one of Ireland's longest-serving Toyota dealerships (over forty years) has impressive showrooms on the main road at Williamstown, although it describes itself as being in Blackrock. It has an extensive range of Toyota cars and commercial vehicles, while it also specialises in pre-used vehicles. Its service department is in Deansgrange Business Park.

CARYSFORT GLASS AND GLAZING

This supplier of all types of glass and glazing materials is based at 86 Carysfort Avenue.

CLONEY AUDIO

This high-quality audio supplier started in Blackrock back in 1966 and ever since, it has continued to develop its reputation as one of the best audio equipment suppliers in the country, adapting to all the changes in audio technology over the years.

CLOTHES RETAILERS

Blackrock has more clothing retailers, especially for women, than any other comparable area in the country. Close to twenty retailers of women's fashions are based in Blackrock, while three retailers cater for men and a similar number for children.

Some of the women's fashions are sold by shops that are part of a chain, such as Pamela Scott, Lisa Perkins and Next. Many of the others are individually owned shops, such as Fran and Jane, Foxrock Fillies, the Blue Boutique and Monica Peters. Among the best-known and regarded fashion boutiques in Blackrock is Khan's on Main Street.

Men's outfitters include Gentlemen Please on Main Street, which sells both trendy and classic styles for men. Retailers of children's clothes include Adams in the Frascati shopping centre and Next in the Blackrock shopping centre. Milupa in Deansgrange Business Park in Blackrock sells children's shoes.

DUBRAY BOOKS

Dubray Books is one of the best-known Irish bookstore chains and it opened in Blackrock shopping centre in 2003 when it acquired the Bookstop outlets there and in the Dún Laoghaire shopping centre. The Blackrock shop is now one of its busiest, with a commendable range of fiction and non-fiction.

FINDLATER'S

Findlater's shop on Main Street, complete with its gigantic clock on the facade, traded in Blackrock from 1879 until 1969.

When the shop opened, it had the first telephone number in Blackrock – appropriately, Blackrock 1. In the late 1940s, the shop was completely remodelled. For many years, right through until the 1960s, the manager was Billy Vaughan, known far and wide for his booming voice. The shop was noted for its extensive selection of groceries, wines and spirits, but it was always counter service. By the 1960s, self-service supermarkets were starting to make big inroads into the Irish grocery trade, helping to finish off Findlater's in the process. The Findlater family, who owned the Blackrock store and many others in the greater Dublin area, had a close connection with the Blackrock area, since they lived close to the top of Newtownpark Avenue for many years.

AIDAN FITZGERALD HAIR SALON

This salon on Main Street caters for both men and women, with services including a wig boutique. It has long been regarded as one of the top such salons in Ireland. Aidan Fitzgerald and his wife Karen Whelan have been running it for over thirty years, during which time they and it have won many prizes and accolades. They purchased the premises in 1981, then spent nine months renovating them before opening for business in June 1982.

FORMER EUROPA CARS

The former Mazda Europa Cars showroom and workshops were a familiar sight on Newtown Avenue, just before the junction with Seafield Avenue, for many years. They had been converted from the old tram depot that once stood here. The 0.5-hectare site was put on the market in 2015 for infill residential development.

FRASCATI MOTORS

This VW and Audi group specialist was started in 2010 by Jason Thomas and Andrew Simpson in the former O'Leary's bakery premises on Sweetman's Avenue. The firm has the latest in diagnostic and other equipment. Other motor firms in the area include Hills Motors in Bath Place, and Donnelly's Tyres and Batteries on George's Avenue.

FRASCATI SHOPPING CENTRE

Major redevelopment and extension works at the Frascati Shopping Centre should be completed by early 2019, doubling its size to 16,000m^2. The cost of this work has been put at €30 million. The centre was acquired by Invesco in 2015.

Present tenants include An Post, Bannon Jewellery, Bookstation, Boots, Debenhams, Peter Mark, Marks &

Spencer, McDonalds, Pamela Scott, The Health Store, Vienna Shoes and Vodafone. When the redevelopment is completed, scheduled to be in 2019 at the time of writing, one of the new tenants will be Aldi, the discount grocery chain. The new-look centre will have an additional twenty-four retailers as well as five extra food and beverage retailers. Existing tenants have taken new or additional space, while the new tenants will also occupy substantial space, all in anticipation of a much increased footfall of shoppers once the centre is completed. It will also have 550 car parking spaces. Major internal refurbishment is taking place while a new glazed roof is being added.

GREHAN'S BUTCHERS

Grehan's was an old-fashioned butchers that traded from a shop at the corner of Main Street and Bath Place; the shop was very distinctive looking, with the lower part of the front facade, below the large plate glass windows, covered in old-fashioned tiling. The shop has long since been replaced by a branch of the

EBS building society, having closed down in the 1980s – the last butcher's shop on Main Street. The tiling is still there, however.

ITALIAN TASTES

Blackrock was well ahead of its time in its taste for continental food; in the 1940s, at 25 Main Street, Michael O'Reilly ran an emporium dedicated to Italian provisions.

JOHNSTON'S SHOP

Johnston's shop, which sold a wide range of newspapers, magazines and confectionery, was next door to the Ulster Bank on Main Street, and was a well-known and frequented shop in the 1970s.

KHAN'S BOUTIQUE

Khan's Boutique has been a fixture of Blackrock's Main Street since 1994 and continues to thrive by selling international fashion brands such as Armani and Versace, as well as featuring the work of noted Irish fashion designers such as Mariad Whisker and Róisín Linnane. The shop is owned by Deryn Mackay and has been so successful that it has doubled in size. When the recession hit Ireland in 2008, Mackay expanded by going more into daywear and accessories. Sadly, a similar boutique that she set up in Mullingar in 2007 did not survive the recession and closed down in 2012, unlike the Blackrock outlet, which has weathered all storms and continued expanding.

FRANK KEANE MOTORS

This well-known motor dealer took over what had been Maxwell Motors, which was equally popular in the Blackrock area, in 2011. The Day family had entered the motor retailing business in 1938, based just off the Blackrock bypass. Maxwell Motors was noted for BMW cars, for which it had a franchise for nineteen years, until 2008. During the recession, the firm got into financial difficulties and went into receivership, but since taking over, Frank Keane has put these Blackrock car showrooms back on the right track.

KENNY'S CENTRA

Kenny's Centra supermarket is the only supermarket on Main Street in Blackrock, at No. 26.

Jim Kenny was brought up over the pub owned by his father and mother at Mary Street in central Dublin, but he and his family have been living in Blackrock since 1982, the same year he married his wife, Kerry. They have been running the supermarket ever since and have now been joined in the business by their sons, Blaise and Desmond. It has long been a Centra store and Kenny says that, so far, they have changed the layout and style of the supermarket three times to meet changing consumer trends. It is noted for its wide selection of foods, its deli and its takeaway coffee.

Kenny also says that about a decade ago, he joined the Unique Blackrock Traders. It had a committee of eight, but three people, including himself, did all the work, and when the other two people left the district, he lost interest in the venture.

ELENA T. KOLEVA

Elena Koleva runs a health and beauty salon above the Newtownpark Pharmacy at No. 3 Newtown Park, just off Newtownpark Avenue. She is a qualified Swedish and sports massage therapist, and says that her staff are very friendly and able to help people attain better health and fitness. However, she says that after ten years in Ireland and more than five running her salon, she is now going to return to her native Bulgaria.

MACKEN'S PHARMACY

Also specialising in health and beauty products, this pharmacy has been based at the corner of Main Street and Carysfort Avenue since 1951. The superintendent pharmacist is Lorcan Macken.

NEWTOWN SHOPPING CENTRE

This small centre on Newtownpark Avenue houses a number of retailers, including O'Brien's off-licence, a branch of Paddy Power the bookmakers, the Moon Oriental takeaway, a barber's shop, a laundry and dry cleaners, and the Blue Orchid restaurant. One of the smallest shopping centres in the Dublin area, it also has a complex of six apartments.

NEWTOWNPARK PHARMACY

Newtownpark Pharmacy, at No. 3 Newtown Park, just off Newtownpark Avenue, is a long-established, family-owned community pharmacy that has been trading since 1956. It serves both Blackrock and Stillorgan, and is well regarded by its customers for being well-stocked and having friendly staff.

OLD BUTCHER

One of the old-style butcher's shops that used to thrive on Blackrock's Main Street was the pork butcher's run by German-born August Horlacker at 2C Main Street in the 1940s.

OLD SHOE REPAIR SHOP

The old shoe repair shop at 62 Carysfort Avenue has long since been converted into a private residence, but the old shop window that jutted on to the pavement is still there, although closed off.

OLD SHOPS

The late Frank Kelly, actor, often used to reminisce about some of the old shops in Blackrock, where he grew up and where he lived for most of his life. Born in 1938, he remembered vividly the horse-drawn carts in Blackrock village, belonging to, among other firms, the local Mooney's Dairy and to Johnston, Mooney and O'Brien's bakery at Ballsbridge.

In terms of local bakeries and shops selling bread, he recalled Mrs Bennett's shop opposite the old library in Blackrock; it was famous in the locality for its brown bread. O'Leary's bakery was originally close to the junction on Main Street and right

beside the ancient cross in its original location. The bakery was eventually replaced by the Central Café, which is today Sisi @ Central Café.

Kelly also remembered O' Neill's the chemists on Main Street, while there was also Willoughby's bicycle shop on George's Avenue. The eccentric mechanic who worked there, George Broadford, used to address what he thought was the whole of Blackrock in a loud, theatrical voice, standing at the door of the shop.

PERMANENT TSB

Permanent TSB closed its retail branch in Blackrock in 2010, but it retains its administrative office on Carysfort Avenue. Other long-established banks in Blackrock continue with their branches in the village: AIB, Bank of Ireland and the Ulster Bank.

PRONTAPRINT

Blackrock once had a thriving Prontaprint instant print shop at Temple Road; the site is now occupied by two takeaway shops.

Frank Sweeney, a lawyer, bought the Prontaprint master franchise in Ireland in 1980. It came with one franchisee, Bob Coe, a former production manager with *The Irish Times* who at that stage had already started his shop in Blackrock. The master franchise lasted until 1988, when it was sold following Sweeney's death.

The Sweeney family lived on Seapoint Avenue, and later in Monkstown. Frank Sweeney's son, Brody, is well-known in business circles. When his father died, he decided not to continue with the printing business, but instead set up O'Brien's sandwich bars. After O'Brien's folded during the great recession (it has since returned), Brody went on to found the Camile Thai chain of restaurants, both in Ireland and in England, and they are successfully trading today. He still has fond memories of growing up as a child on Seapoint Avenue.

QUINN & BYRNE

Quinn & Byrne was one of the old-style grocery shops in Blackrock, long gone, at 2 Main Street. It reached the apex of its fortunes in the early 1950s and was also an off-licence, selling a wide range of wines and spirits. Another wine retailer at that time, also long gone, was Gilbey's at 21 Main Street.

At around the same time, Lipton's, a branch of a well-known English chain, had an extensive shop in Blackrock, at 5 to 9 Main Street. In the 1950s and '60s, Lipton's had around sixty shops in this part of Ireland, but at the end of the

1960s, as supermarket competition intensified, the Lipton's shops disappeared like snow in a heatwave. Yet another long-disappeared chain of food shops, Blanchardstown Mills, also had an outlet in the 1950s in Blackrock, at 37 Main Street. Again, it was well ahead of its time, as most of its foodstuffs were presented loose, in bulk displays.

RAVEN BOOKS

Yet another Blackrock bookseller, Raven Books is based at 34 Main Street. The bookshop was started by Louisa Cameron, on Carysfort Avenue, in 2008; she subsequently moved the shop to Main Street, where it continues as a small, independent bookshop, with a good general mix of new and second-hand books. It is regarded as being one of the best independent booksellers in the Dublin area.

ROCHES STORES

Roches Stores had a long and contentious relationship with Blackrock.

The founder, William Roche, a farmer's son from Co Cork, set up his first shop in Cork city in 1901, selling furniture. It survived the Black and Tan raids and the burning of Cork city centre. By the end of the 1920s, Roche had bought his first Dublin store, at Henry Street, and went on a decade later to open his first store in Limerick. However, the family was always secretive in its dealings, and by the 1970s had re-registered the company in the Isle of Man so that it never had to publish its accounts in Ireland.

The real battle for Roche's Stores came in Blackrock. Frescati House was built in 1739 for the family of John Hely Hutchinson, the then Provost of Trinity College. In the 1750s, the house was sold to the Fitzgerald family for use as a summer residence in the country. They subsequently spent a vast sum of money, £65,000, extending and enhancing the house. The exterior was austere, but the interiors were richly decorated and its lands stretched back to what is now Sydney Avenue. It was the favourite house of Lord Edward Fitzgerald, a key nationalist revolutionary and United Irishman in late eighteenth-century Ireland

Fast-forward to 1970, when Roches Stores bought the house and estate. Over the next thirteen years, they let the house fall into ruin. Despite a battle with conservationists that lasted thirteen years, the house was demolished in the early hours of 4 November 1983 by a company controlled by Roches Stores. They subsequently built a shopping centre on the site, complete with a large branch of Roches Stores.

The retailer put up a plaque commemorating Frescati House, but it contained a spelling error. The house was named as Frascati House, so ever since, it has been the Frascati shopping centre.

Roches Stores sold out to Debenhams in 2006 and its stores have long since disappeared. In 2015, Invesco, a global property investment company, bought the centre for €68 million and is in the middle of a huge expansion plan for the centre, which should be completed in 2019.

SPAR

The Spar supermarket on the lower part of Newtownpark Avenue has traded as Spar for close to twenty years, and before that was an independent grocery shop.

SUE RYDER

This shop at 10A Carysfort Avenue is run by the Sue Ryder Foundation, a not-for-profit organisation dedicated to helping those with terminal illnesses and neurological conditions.

SUNWAY TRAVEL

For many years, Sunway Travel, the largest Irish-owned tour operator, was based in its shop on Main Street, Blackrock, directly opposite the old post office.

The firm was founded by Roy Beatty in 1966; it then passed to his daughter, Madeline Kilbride, in 1974, and finally to his granddaughter, Tanya Airey, in 1998. For the first twenty-five years of its existence, Sunway was a corporate and leisure travel agent, before it started tour operations to Morocco in 1991. Since then, the firm, long since based in Dún Laoghaire, has greatly expanded its operations, including through a number of takeovers. Tanya Airey remains chief executive, while her father, Jim Furlong, has been chairman since 1974. Tanya's husband Philip is a director, while her cousin, Brian McGowan, is the financial controller. So while Sunway Travel is now a big name in the Irish travel business, it remains very much a family firm.

THE NEST

The Nest was a delightful small sweet shop up a flight of steps at 84 Carysfort Avenue, just before the turn into Brookfield Avenue. It was owned and run for many years by the Williams family. For much of the second half of the twentieth century, it was listed in Thom's Directories, going strong as far back as 1960, and was still listed in 1986. The shop has now been transformed into a private residence on this terrace of houses.

ULSTER BANK

The Ulster Bank branch on Main Street in Blackrock, close to the junction with Carysfort Avenue, is by far the oldest bank in Blackrock, dating back to its construction in 1892. Other bank branches in Blackrock, including AIB and Bank of Ireland, are far more modern in construction.

14

SPORT

AVOCA HOCKEY CLUB

The Avoca Hockey Club was started in 1891 as part of Avoca School, but was re-established in 1929 to provide a place for past pupils of the school to continue playing hockey after they left. After Avoca School was merged with Kingstown Grammar School in 1973 to form Newtownpark Comprehensive School, the club was expanded to cater for past pupils of Newtownpark. The club is affiliated to the Leinster branch of the Irish Hockey Association.

Over the years, the club has won many prizes for men's and women's as well as indoor hockey. Currently, it has three men's teams and four women's teams, as well as an active veterans' team and a youth section. All the senior teams play in the Leinster League.

BLACKROCK ATHLETIC CLUB

Founded in 1944, Blackrock Athletic is one of the largest juvenile clubs in Dublin. Unlike many similar clubs, which have either folded or been forced to amalgamate, it has withstood the test of time.

Based at Carysfort Park in Blackrock, it caters for athletes at both junior and senior level. The junior section is intended for athletes aged from 8 to 18, and it has a current membership of around 100. The junior section also has academy training for 6- and 7-year-olds, which is run by the parents of that age group.

The club colours date back to 1946, while the club crest is two years younger, designed in 1948 by Dick Cahill, one of the early committee members. It represents the golden wings of morning, denoting speed, and encircling the rising sun, which is sending forth its golden rays, a symbol of youth and freshness.

BLACKROCK BOWLING AND TENNIS CLUB

This venerable sporting club dates back to 1906. The club is in a tranquil setting on Green Road, just off Mount Merrion Avenue, where its facilities include four all-weather tennis courts and a brand new, state-of-the-art bowling green, built to USPGA specifications. The club also has excellent changing facilities.

The large hall is used for indoor bowling and can also be used by members for a wide range of social functions. Fees range from €320 a year for senior bowlers, with a €20 discount for over 65s, to junior tennis at €50 per annum with a senior member. Coaching is available for all junior members, from age 5 upwards.

BLACKROCK COLLEGE

Blackrock College and sport have been synonymous for close on 140 years.

The rugby club at the college was founded in 1882 and it has become one of the foremost senior rugby clubs in Ireland. Since 1961, the college's rugby football club has been based at Stradbrook, on the opposite side of Blackrock to the college.

Altogether, some forty of the best-known names in Irish rugby are past pupils of Blackrock College, including Ryle Nugent, now an RTÉ rugby commentator, Gary Ringrose and Fergus Slattery. See the *Old Boys' Club* subsections of Chapter 10 for more.

Former students who have achieved success in other sports include Nicholas Roche (professional cycling), Michael Darragh MacAuley, Cian O'Sullivan and Mark Vaughan, all Dublin GAA footballers.

Besides rugby, Blackrock College has an excellent record in other sports, including athletics, swimming, table tennis, tennis and water polo. Squash and cricket are other specialities, as well as basketball, cross country-running and golf, while Blackrock College also has a commendable record in Gaelic games, football and hurling.

BLACKROCK COLLEGE'S GAA PROWESS

While Blackrock College may be known far and wide for the ease with which it produces rugby stars, it has also long had a strong GAA tradition, which continues to this day.

One person who played a key role in the college's GAA revival was Brendan O'Regan, the man who did so much to put Shannon airport on the map, including with its duty free and tax free zone initiatives. Brought up in a strong GAA family, he had come to Blackrock College in 1931 as a 14-year-old boarder. Some years before that, Blackrock College had played in the Leinster Colleges' hurling competition, but had then dropped out.

Brendan O'Regan gathered together some of his school friends and they all went to see Dr John Charles McQuaid, then president of the college. They requested that Blackrock College return to these hurling matches and McQuaid approved. In 1932/33, a junior team that included O'Regan entered the hurling competition and began a decade-long golden era for the sport at Blackrock. In the first three years after they returned to the competition, Blackrock College won both the junior and senior trophies.

Eventually, howeer, the college's participation in intercollegiate hurling fizzled out. After heavy defeats in the senior competition in 1937 and 1938, and the transfer out of the college of various priests who had been hurling coaches, interest waned, and by 1942, the golden era of hurling at Blackrock was over.

CARRAIG TENNIS CLUB

Based at Rockfield Park, Carraig Tennis Club has a total of five public courts, all lit.

ST AUGUSTINE'S SHARKS SPECIAL OLYMPICS

This is a small club for pupils and past pupils of St Augustine's school in Blackrock. It has three coaches and about thirty-six athletes with mild special needs. The club meets on Mondays and Tuesdays during term time for forty-five-minute sessions. At the 2018 national finals of the Ireland Games for special needs sportspeople, members of the club brought back several golds and silvers.

ST OLAF'S GAA CLUB

The St Olaf's GAA club, based at Holly Avenue in Stillorgan Business Park, serves a wide area of south Dublin, including Blackrock. It is a welcoming club, respecting diversity and encouraging juveniles, men and women of all abilities and backgrounds to take part in its sporting activities. It fields teams in football, women's football, hurling and camogie.

15

TRANSPORT

BLACKROCK BYPASS

The Blackrock bypass was opened by Councillor Anne Brady on 24 March 1988, and it was designed to divert through-traffic away from Main Street. However, it has also had the effect of cutting Blackrock in two, separating the shops and other facilities in Main Street from the rest of Blackrock. The two big shopping centres in the district were built on either side of the bypass.

BLACKROCK RAILWAY STATION

The railway station at Blackrock opened with the beginning of the new railway line from Westland Row to Dunleary at the end of 1834. It was designed by John Skipton Mulvany (1813–70) to look like a small, classical-style villa. He also designed a canopy, supported by pillars, for the platform nearest to Blackrock village. The platform on the seaward side of the station wasn't afforded any such protection from the elements. Mulvany also designed the Salthill and Monkstown station, which opened in 1837. Another of his masterpieces was the Broadstone railway station in Dublin, the terminus for the Midland & Great Western station, which closed to rail traffic in 1937 and which is now the headquarters of Bus Éireann.

For most of the 1930s until the late '40s, Blackrock also saw plenty of evidence of another railway revolution, the Drumm battery-operated trains, which operated between Dublin and Bray. The Drumm trains were way ahead of their time, fast and efficient and entirely dependent on their batteries for motive power. The system was scrapped in the late 1940s, mainly because spare parts had become impossible to obtain. In the late 1950s and early '60s, Blackrock saw the nationwide switch from steam to diesel on the railways, while in 1984 yet another transport revolution came to Blackrock when the DART electrified system began operations. It continues to this day as a mainstay of the commuter traffic to and from Blackrock.

It is a sign of the revolutionary impact of the first railway that when the lovely seaside Idrone Terrace was built in the 1840s, close to Blackrock railway station, the houses there were built with no stables for horses. Ever since then, trains have played an important part in sustaining Blackrock as an integral part of the greater Dublin commuter belt.

BLACKROCK TUNNEL

On the railway line through Blackrock, there is one solitary tunnel, all of 21m long. Before the line was built, there were proposals for an additional tunnel beneath the grounds of Lord Cloncurry's residence, Maretimo House, at Seapoint, with pedestrian bridges at either end. However, these bridges were never built, although another footbridge across the line, with striking towers at either end, was constructed and still stands today. As for Maretimo House, this was demolished in 1970.

Mulvany also lived in Blackrock for a short time, at Cross Avenue, from 1843 to 1845. He moved on to Seapoint for a further two years.

BUSES

Blackrock is served by a total of nine bus routes, including one cross-city route, the 17, which runs from Blackrock railway station to Rialto. A major shake-up of the Dublin bus network is due to come into effect later in 2019 and it is planned that the many changes will include a far greater frequency on bus routes through Blackrock.

CYCLE ROUTE

A 5km-long cycle route runs from Blackrock to Dún Laoghaire; closer to Dublin, cyclists have to share the bus lanes through Merrion. The cycle route starts at Booterstown DART station; from Blackrock DART station, it progresses to Idrone Terrace, before joining a contra-flow trail on Newtown Avenue. The cycle trail then joins traffic at Seapoint Avenue and concludes at Dún Laoghaire harbour.

Blackrock also has a reasonable amount of parking facilities for cyclists, although in 2013 a planned upgrade to the Blackrock bypass was described as creating extra risks for both cyclists and pedestrians. At the time of writing, discussion continues about improvements to cycling tracks in the Blackrock area, but with no clear indication as to when they'll be implemented.

For well over a decade now, plans have been progressed for the s2s cycle route to run from Sandycove to Sutton, along the shores of Dublin Bay. Further new plans for this cycle route were announced in May 2018, including a new section from Blackrock to Seapoint. Parts of the s2s route are already open, including the section at Dollymount, which opened in 2017.

DART

The DART electrified rapid transit system started in 1984 and ever since it has been a vital link for commuters living in Blackrock and travelling to the city centre. The DART system goes as far as Bray and Greystones on the southside of the city and to Malahide and Howth on the northside. Long-distance trains from Dublin to Rosslare pass through Blackrock station, but don't stop there.

FIRST RECORDED TRAFFIC ACCIDENT

The first recorded traffic accident in the Blackrock area took place in 1743, when a local cleric, the Rev Heney, and his wife, were travelling in a horse-drawn chaise between Booterstown and Blackrock. The horse managed to turn off the road and it and the chaise fell down what was described as a 'great precipice'. Fortunately, the reverend gentleman and his wife managed to leap out and escaped, shocked but unhurt, but the unfortunate horse was killed when it hit the bottom of the ravine and the chaise was smashed into pieces.

JAUNTING CARS AND TRAMS

Before the advent of tram services from Dublin to Blackrock and from Blackrock to what was then Kingstown, the usual method of road transport was by horse-drawn jaunting cars.

These had been in use since the early eighteenth century, and by the end of that century, they were a well-established, indeed the only means, of getting from Dublin to Blackrock. One of the main operators was based in Ringsend and prices from 1792 show that in that year the charge for taking a coach from Ringsend to Blackrock was 3*s* 6*d*, while a horse-drawn charabanc cost 2*s* 4*d*. The cheapest form of transport was a chaise, which cost 1*s* 4*d*.

After the opening of the Westland Row to Dunleary rail line in 1834, residential development began in earnest close to the railway line, including in Blackrock. Eventually, the Dublin Southern Districts Tramways company got permission to build a tram line from Blackrock to Haddington Road, which opened in 1879; it used double-deck trams that were horse-drawn. Later on, it became possible to travel by tram all the way from Dublin city centre, through Blackrock to Dalkey, although the journey meant two changes. When the railway was extended through Dalkey, the same journey could be made by train in a quarter of the time.

In 1882, in order to try and compete with the railway, the Dublin Southern Districts Tramways company introduced steam trams on the route to Blackrock. These ran for just over two years and were then abandoned, partly because of all the complaints from residents living close to the line. A rival tramway, the Blackrock and Kingstown tram company, was set up in 1884. By the early years of the twentieth century, Dublin's tramways had been amalgamated into the Dublin

United Tramways company, which also electrified all its routes. The No. 6 tram ran from Nelson's Pillar, by the GPO, to Blackrock. In those days, as so many people were illiterate, the tram routes were also designated by symbols. For the trams going to Blackrock and on as far as Dalkey, a green symbol like a three-leaf clover was used. The other tram routes that ran through Blackrock were the 7 and the 8.

From the 1930s, the tram company began to use many more buses, and and by 1941, double-decker buses had replaced an equal number of trams in the Dublin area. Eventually, in 1945, the Dublin tramway company and nearly all railway services around the country were amalgamated into a new company, CIE. Five years later, in 1950, it was nationalised. The last tram service in the Dublin area, from the city centre to Dalkey, the No. 8, closed down on 9 July 1949. The old tram depot in Blackrock was turned into the Mazda Europa Cars centre, which itself was subsequently demolished.

PARKING

Car parking in Blackrock village has long been a problem, made worse as car ownership in the area has become almost universal; bicycle parking is less of a drawback.

Parking for cars close to Main Street remains very difficult, although there is some close to Blackrock DART station, but this is mainly used by commuters. The two shopping centres in Blackrock also have car parks, but apart from that, parking can be extremely difficult. The Blackrock Business Network proposed a number of remedies in July 2018 that, if implemented, could help alleviate the problem.

ROCK ROAD

Rock Road, which forms the main approach to Blackrock coming from the Dublin city direction, is one of the oldest roads in the country, the Slighe Chualann. Dating back about 2,000 years, it was one of five roads that radiated from the Hill of Tara in Co Meath, where the High Kings of Ireland were based. Rock Road ran from the Hill as far as Co Wicklow. The sheer volume of traffic on this main road now far exceeds anything dreamed of by the original makers of the roads. Well over 20,000 cars, vans, trucks and buses use Rock Road every weekday.

16

WORK

AN POST

An Post opened its sorting office in Blackrock Business Park, off Carysfort Avenue (the site of the old Glen Abbey hosiery factory) in 1988. Before it opened, local sorting had been done in the sorting room, which was at the back of the old post office on Main Street. Currently, the An Post organisation is involved in a major slimming down and restructuring operation.

BLACKROCK CREDIT UNION

The Blackrock Credit Union was founded in 1970 and began in premises on Temple Road; initially, it had twelve members. It is now based at 1 Carysfort Avenue, where Conn Collins is the general manager, and has 4,500 members. One of its recent developments was the launch of its new website in June 2017.

BLACKROCK GLASS

Blackrock Glass, which is based at Grange Terrace, Blackrock, is an Irish-owned, family-run company with two generations of glass experts. It was set up thirty-five years ago and has a team of ten experts who install the most contemporary systems and products, including glass balustrades and double glazing.

BLACKHALL PUBLISHING

Blackhall Publishing was incorporated in December 1996. For just over ten years now, it has been based at Avoca Avenue in Blackrock; before then, it was on Carysfort Avenue.

The firm specialises in codification and electronic publishing services, especially for the legal profession. It is a specialist in law consolidation and the preparation of reports.

DBA PUBLICATIONS AND DESIGN

Producing a wide variety of publications as well as providing top-rate design services, this company, which was founded by Des Donegan in 1986, is now owned by Tadhg Cowhig. It has always been based on Carysfort Avenue.

GLEN ABBEY

For many years, the Glen Abbey company had a textile manufacturing company just off Carysfort Avenue in Blackrock, but it closed down at the end of the 1980s.

The origins of the company date from 1932, when Colm Barnes (1919–2003), from the Falls Road in Belfast, came to Dublin and set up a knitwear company. Then, with his brother Rory, he started a clothes manufacturing business in

Clanbrassil Street. At the end of the Second World War, the company bought a disused First World War airfield in Tallaght and built a factory there, which, in 1957, was renamed Glen Abbey Textiles. By the end of the 1960s the company was also manufacturing women's hosiery in Blackrock and employed over 1,000 people, 70 per cent of whom were female. But by 1983, the company was trading at a loss because of increased international competition in the Irish market. That same year, Glen Abbey was sold to a well-known entrepreneur, John Teeling, later to become renowned in the whiskey distilling business.

The site of Glen Abbey's old factory in Blackrock was turned into the Blackrock Business Park, and at the end of 2004, planning permission was given to build substantial office accommodation there.

KRAFT HEINZ

The Irish arm of this global, American-owned food giant relocated its headquarters for Ireland to the newly refurbished Avoca Court in Blackrock in 2018.

MARTELLO PRESS

Situated at Brookfield Avenue, off Carysfort Avenue, Martello Press was established in 1987 by Joseph and Margaret Byrne. It has been on Brookfield Avenue since 1989 and specialises in four-colour litho print, as well as A3 digital and wide-format digital printing. The firm is also noted for having printed many books over the years.

MODERN OFFICES

By the early 1990s, Blackrock had become the location of choice in the greater Dublin area outside Dublin city for the offices of commercial companies. Many insurance and other companies relocated to Blackrock, such as Zurich Insurance, which established its Irish headquarters in Blackrock.

In addition to so many commercial companies making their Irish base in Blackrock, by 2000, a total of twenty computer-related companies had relocated to Blackrock, and in the nearly two decades since, that trend has accelerated.

NEWTOWNPARK DAIRYMEN AND FARMERS

The Newtownpark area was noted in the nineteenth and early twentieth centuries for the number of farmers, including dairy farmers, and dairymen it sustained.

Local cattlemen and dairies included James and Thomas Calvert, the Costigan family, Thomas Dunbar, John Jolly, O'Malleys at St Ita's, George Sutton, John Valentine, also of St Ita's and the Wexford Dairy in Newtownpark village. Up until the 1950s, dairy farms in the area delivered milk door to door, but that trade was taken over by larger dairies. These days, of course, it is most unusual for milk to be home-delivered since it is usually bought in shops or supermarkets.

The big dairy company in the area was once the Tel el Kebir dairy. Its unusual name came from a member of the Sutton family who was in the British Army and took part in the Battle of Tel el Kebir in Egypt, in 1882, when he made a name for himself by saving the regimental colours. When he retired from military service in 1884, he came home to south Dublin and set up a small dairy company. It continued to expand in the early twentieth century, introducing pasteurisation in 1926. At that stage, however, its milk came not from the Newtownpark area but from counties Wexford and Wicklow.

NURSING AND MIDWIFERY BOARD

Based on Carysfort Avenue, this board supports registered nurses and midwives in providing patient care to the highest of standards.

RGDATA

RGDATA is the organisation that represents independent retailers in Ireland. Despite the onslaught of supermarkets in Ireland, there are still 4,000 independent retailers represented by the organisation. For many years, it was based in offices on Main Street in Blackrock, although it is now in Deansgrange. Its director-general, since 2006, is Tara Buckley.

SOUTHSIDE PARTNERSHIP

Based in offices beside the old post office on Main Street, Southside Partnership deals with social problems, including exclusion, in the wider Dún Laoghaire-Rathdown county council area.

THE GLOSS

The Gloss fashion magazine, which is published monthly with *The Irish Times*, was started in 2005 by two sisters, Jane and Sarah McDonald. In addition to *The Gloss*, other publications, in print and digital format, are produced.

Jane McDonald worked in the fashion business in London but returned to Dublin to take over the editorship of Kevin Kelly's *Image* magazine. In 1999, she passed the editorship to her sister Sarah and became the managing director of Image Publications, although she retained the editor's job at *Image Interiors*. Someone else who had close connections with *Image* was Tracy Ormiston, who is the advertising director of *The Gloss*.

A year after *The Gloss* was founded, *The Irish Times* invested in the magazine. The early years were financially challenging, but these days it is doing well, with considerable volumes of advertising from high-profile brands aimed at well-to-do women. Despite the split from *Image*, that magazine's then-owner, Kevin Kelly, subsequently made an unsolicited offer to buy out *The Gloss*, but he was turned down.

The Gloss has always been based at The Courtyard, 40 Main Street, Blackrock, but it wasn't the first fashion publisher in either Main Street or Blackrock. *Futura* magazine got there first, in 1964, when it started as a trade magazine for women's fashions, expanding into other areas such as footwear, sportswear, menswear and children's wear, even leather goods.

RECOMMENDED READING

Between the Mountains and the Sea by Peter Pearson (Dublin, 1998)

Blackrock in Old Photographs by Joe Curtis (Dublin, 2014)

Blackrock College, Fearless and Bold edited by Paddy Murray (London, 2009)

Blackrock College, 1860–1995, by Fr Séan Farragher (Dublin, 1995)

Book of Blackrock by John L. O' Sullivan and Séamus Cannon (Blackrock, 1987)

The Book of Blackrock by Liam Mac Cóil (Blackrock, 1977)

Guide to Blackrock, Co Dublin by Rev George Thomas Stokes (Dublin, 1892)

Hidden Stream, a new history of Dún Laoghaire-Rathdown by Brian MacAongusa (Dublin, 2007)

Hill's Guide to Blackrock, Dublin, 1892, facsimile edition (Blackrock, 1976)

Newtownpark Avenue, its people and their houses, by Cornelius F. Smith (Dublin, 2001)

Our Lady of Mercy College, Blackrock, no author given, (Dublin, 1986)